MAKING PEACE *with* MOTHERHOOD...
and CREATING A BETTER YOU

Heidi Bratton

PAULIST PRESS
New York/Mahwah, N.J.

Cover design by Cynthia Dunne
Cover and photographs on pp. 83 and 100 by Heidi Bratton
Text design by Lynn Else

Library of Congress Cataloging-in-Publication Data

Bratton, Heidi.
    Making peace with motherhood—and creating a better you / Heidi Bratton.
        p. cm.
    Includes bibliographical references.
    ISBN 0-8091-4076-4
    1. Mothers—Religious life. 2. Motherhood—Religious aspects—Christianity.
I. Title.

    BV4529.18 .B73 2002
    248.8'431—dc21

                                                                2002003642

Published by Paulist Press
997 Macarthur Boulevard
Mahwah, New Jersey 07430

www.paulistpress.com

Printed and bound in the
United States of America

Dedication

For my daughter, Nicole, and my son, Peter, whose births sent me down this mothering path and who brought me cookie dough for nourishment when I was wedded to my computer during final revisions of this book.

For my daughters, Olivia and Lucy, and my son, Benjamin, who gave me a second chance at mothering and whose not-so-quiet, laughing feet snuck past Daddy, "found" me hiding at my computer, and "surprised" me with hugs.

You are my parade and my pride and joy. Never has a mother been so blessed as I am with each of you. I love you all to the moon, the stars, and everywhere.

Also by Heidi Bratton
Published by Paulist Press

Count Your Blessings

Imagine

Little Ways To Give God Praise

Rejoice! Jesus Welcomes Me!

Spirit!

The Little Shepherd

Where Is God?

Yes I Can!

Table of Contents

Acknowledgments

The cast of characters that has brought this book to life is a large and joyous one. Primarily, I owe this book to my husband, John. It was with his undying encouragement that this mother found her voice and began to speak; this photographer learned to paint with words as well as light. I owe an immeasurable debt to him for being my first reader and my computer technician, for proudly showing my books off to colleagues at work, for not letting me give up, and for believing in the message of this book.

The first and final drafts are marvelously different because of former Paulist Press publisher, Kevin Lynch, C.S.P., who let me read perceptive comments from reviewers; current Paulist Press publisher, Lawrence Boadt, C.S.P., who saw the manuscript's potential and championed it; and my current Paulist Press editor, Joseph Scott, C.S.P., whose suggestions both tightened and enlarged the book's point of view. The contributions of each, although invisible to readers, filled my thoughts and therefore my writing with the need for grace as well as peace.

I am blessed to have a sister and a brother-in-law like Wendy and Francis Hyatt. Their support was the foundation of this book. I am particularly grateful to my parents, Don and Carolyn Egan. From the very beginning, they believed in my ability to become a good mother. Over the years they have sent many cartoons, books, gifts, flowers, faxes, fall leaves, cookies, and copies—and I know that each time it was their way of wrapping up a little love and sending it my way. Mom and Dad, I love you and like you, too. I thank my in-laws, Kevin and Pinky Bratton, whose generosity has blessed our family time and again and made it largely possible for their son and me to pursue some pretty lofty dreams.

Many thanks are due to my sister-in-law, Tami Bratton, the real writer in our family. Had she not cleverly titled my first big talk on mothering "At Home Balancing Babies and Business," this whole thing might never have gotten off the ground. My brother, Dale Egan, provided me with much needed legal counsel, sharing his time and expertise with his naïve big sister.

I am indebted to the beautiful women who have shared their mothering journeys with me, enriching my life and this book with their stories: Marie Thibodeau, Jennifer Snyder, Gayle Heaslip, Carolyn Marquez, Donna Curran, Sherry Matis, Stephanie Kiernan, Joanne Perris, Cathleen Tashjian, and Karen Scialabba. I'm especially grateful to the moms in our couples' Bible Study on Cape Cod: Denise Colosi, Karen Heard, Amy Landry, Siobhan O'Brien, Diane Quinn, and Mary Schruckmayr.

Finally, and yet first of all, thanks be to God the Father, the Son, and the Holy Spirit.

Some mothers appear in this book under their own names. I have changed the names of others to protect confidentiality. All shared with the hope that their experiences might help other women make peace with motherhood. All scripture references are from the New International Version (NIV) unless otherwise noted.

INTRODUCTION

Changing the World One Diaper at a Time

It was our fourth doctor's visit in ten days. A routine physical for my five-year-old daughter, an emergency visit with my nine-year-old daughter after she suffered an asthma attack at school, a reluctant visit for myself to be officially diagnosed with bronchitis, and now, a second reluctant visit for myself which would reveal an inflamed esophagus from my bronchitis pill getting caught in my throat. The days between these visits had been filled with entertaining family from out of town. I was tired, dead tired.

As we sat in the doctor's waiting room my seventeen-month-old son began to make the predictably pained faces and body movements to assure me that yes, indeed, entering a doctor's waiting room had become his signal for having a bowel movement during these last ten days.

"Not now. Not this time, too!" I sighed, as the noxious odor began to raise eyebrows on the other side of the waiting room. Leaving my five- and three-year-old daughters in the care of a sympathetic receptionist, I slung my son over my arm and dashed out to the parking lot. I began a desperate search for one, just one, "Oh, please, God," one diaper stuck somewhere in the giant petri dish of kid stuff fermenting in our family minivan. Of course, I had left my diaper bag at home.

No. None. Zero. Zip. "Argggh!"

"God, if you love me, please! Just one diaper! Would it be too hard for you? You who made the heavens and the earth? Can't you see how tired I am?" I know I'm in a really bad way when I start pleading with God right out loud.

A grandmotherly-type lady peeked in the open van door and asked if she could be of assistance. I smiled that polite, squinty-eyed, tight-lipped smile and shook my head.

"Oh, just changing a diaper. No, really, we're just fine. Thank you anyway. Good-bye." Of course, we both knew differently, but she was either polite enough or frightened enough to leave me alone. By now the baby was screaming bloody murder because I had stripped him naked and pinned him under my forearm in a vain effort to keep his clothes clean. Of course, the emergency change of clothes was in the diaper bag, back home, and this was a messy one. Too much apple juice.

Sparing you the details, I hastily combined divine inspiration and CEO-decision-making power and decided to relieve the fullness of the diaper without eliminating the diaper itself. Confidently collecting my two other children, I marched into the examination room with my little parade and completed the entire appointment without the slightest detection. It fact, the odor had been so reduced that I forgot to change the poor boy until we got back in the van a few hours later and a plastic bag of brown, mushy wipes fell out of the side door!

I know this is too much information for those of you who do not deal with dirty diapers on a daily basis. I will shift from earthly to divine imagery. The Apostle Paul says in Philippians that we are to let our offerings to God be a sweet aroma; our lives are to be a pleasing fragrance to the Lord. How clearly I can picture, after that morning at the doctor's office, that even our smallest actions have a very large impact on the world around us. Doing *something*, as imperfect as it was, made a world of difference—made the air a little sweeter—for the six people crammed in that tiny examination room.

Changing the world one diaper at a time. It is what a loving parent does. It is a philosophy, a belief that even the smallest, most unsavory tasks that I do out of love for my children change them. Change me. Change the environment of our home, our school, our church, our community, our nation, our world. If, out of humble love, like our Lord Jesus who washed his disciples' feet, we embrace the opportunity to serve a child, who cannot repay us, by changing his diaper, by feeding her, by laughing with her or by disciplining him, then one diaper can be the beginning of a revolution.

Making Peace with Motherhood and Creating a Better You is a book about this revolution of the heart, the mind, and the soul. It is an invitation to peace for mothers, at home and working, who want to make some changes in their mothering styles, but are afraid to. Mothers who have chosen to be at home with their children but have lost their identities somewhere in the midst of family responsibilities. Mothers who are hungry for a richer sense of self. Mothers who love their jobs and always said that they were not "cut out" to stay at home with children, but then found themselves crying the day Junior took his first steps at daycare.

In her book *Fruitful*, Anne Roiphe writes, "It is clear to me that feminism, despite its vast accomplishments, has not cured me of motherhood." Only after five children and twelve years of mothering have I come to realize that Roiphe's basic assumption (even if it is metaphorical) is completely wrong. Motherhood is not a disease! Pregnancy is not an illness.

The basic premise of this book is that motherhood is not an obstacle to be overcome or to be avoided on the way to self-realization. Having children is not a punishment but a privilege. As post-modern Christian mothers, we need to make peace with the fact that while having a child may mean that we have to postpone or reshape some of our own goals and ambitions, it doesn't mean that our lives as individuals are over. If God has given you a child, entrusted you with the care of one of his precious lambs, then motherhood is a part of living up to your full potential as a woman.

I only had *one* diaper. And although it desperately needed to be taken off and thrown away, *completely* changed, it wasn't possible. Clearly, dumping the contents and putting the diaper back on wasn't a perfect solution. I wouldn't have received an A+ if I had been taking an exam. But I was able to lessen an unpleasant odor from one that had quickly filled the expanse of a waiting room to one that no one even noticed in the confines of an examination room. I made a difference.

My deepest desire is that some insight I share here in writing or some experiences that you share with other moms as a result of reading this book will encourage you to make peace with *your* motherhood. I want to encourage you to stride confidently, whole-heartedly into motherhood; to choose to make a difference for the child that God has given to you. Look up from the details for a time and see the big picture. You will be able to change the world, use your education, fulfill your dreams by taking life one child, one step, one season, one diaper at a time.

Part I

Reconciling Womanhood and Motherhood

Chapter 1

Bearing Fruit: Defining Godly Expectations

Ideally, I begin my day by snatching a verse from scripture and reflecting on it as I run around the cranberry bogs near our home. Some days the sun rises adorned in pink clouds bestowing rays from the very throne of heaven. Other days the sun flickers awhile just below the darkened skyline like a flame crawling along the edge of a piece of paper until, poof, the fire takes hold and the warmth of morning bursts into the bog. It is a rejuvenating time for me in my spiritual relationship with Jesus and in my relationship with the world in which I will live out the day ahead.

This morning was neither ideal nor rejuvenating. Crawling out of bed at 7:15 A.M., I had completely missed my sunrise time with God and my school-aged kids were going to miss the bus if I didn't get a move on. I was disappointed in myself for being lazy and failing to get up and run.

Later in the day I e-mailed my husband at work and told him to "kick my lazy self out of bed tomorrow so I can go running!" He e-mailed back, "I'd rather have your lazy self help me put away the groceries. Thanks for your help. Take a nap."

I was startled. I had completely forgotten that I had gotten to bed around midnight, late for me, because I had stayed up to help him with the groceries (he does the grocery shopping). After reading his e-mail I also remembered that our eighteen-month-old baby had awakened at 5 A.M. needing to be rocked back to sleep. When dawn beckoned an hour later, I simply couldn't answer the call.

Why was I so disappointed in myself? I had stayed up late and been awakened early. My husband could see that taking a morning run was not a realistic expectation, but I was fixated on what I had *expected* to have happen rather than on what *actually* happened. It was unrealistic and unnecessarily destructive to label myself as lazy for "failing" to get up and run, instead of just expressing disappointment in the circumstances that made me unusually tired. I wasn't lazy at all. I had chosen to put my husband's and my baby's needs ahead of my own. In that specific situation I had made good and reasonable mothering choices.

Unrealistic expectations can go the other way, too. Sometimes we don't get what we expected to have, as when I expected to be able to run, but sometimes we are given gifts we could never even have imagined, much less expected.

For example, we have five children between the ages of two and ten. Matching the number of seat belts available and car seats needed for our young children means that our family barely fits into a mini-van, much less in a mid-sized vehicle. It is a reality that almost made me not want to have more than three children. Really.

When my husband and I talked about the "perfect" family size early in our marriage, I would say, "Well, we can't have more than three children because what if we want to fly somewhere and have to rent a car? With any more than three children we would not be able to fit in a mid-sized rental car. So, three kids is it." My husband was bewildered that I could really allow such a minor detail to so significantly impact a much more important decision.

Okay, okay. So maybe I was micro-managing the whole decision a little bit. At the time, however, I was dead serious. Several years and many trips later, I know *for certain* that having three or fewer kids would make traveling easier, "more perfect," than traveling with our flock of five, but here's the twist: traveling anywhere without them has completely lost its appeal! Today, I'd rather promenade around the block with kids, strollers, pets, toys, friends, and whoever or whatever else should join in, than to fly off to anywhere in the world all by myself—something I could not have anticipated as a newlywed planning the "perfect" family.

Carrie is a mother who was quite satisfied with having two children.

"I never imagined having a large family. It was something that I never really considered. We had two girls aged three years old and fifteen months old at the time my husband asked me, 'What do you think about having a third?' I gave it some thought and within a few months I was pregnant with our third child. Then, at the 21-week ultrasound, we found out that we were expecting twin boys! This meant that I would have four children under the age of five. It was all overwhelming. I worried very much about my two girls and how I would find time for them and the babies. The challenge of meeting the needs of two infants and a two- and four-year-old was very difficult at times, but I never expected how wonderful this large family would be for my children and for me. The benefit to my children of being in a large family continues to amaze me. They learn patience and cooperation. There is always someone to play with. The benefits far out-weigh the concerns I had before the twins were born. God has truly blessed me with the gift of my four children. We are our own parade wherever we go."

Carrie was more or less talked into having a third child and ended up having a third *and* a fourth! She went from a state of contentment with two children, to a state of total disbelief, shock, and worry over how to handle twins, and then to calling herself blessed by God for getting more children than she would have ever expected (or would have planned) to have.

This is the unexpected, unexplainable wonder of having a child that makes motherhood unlike anything I have ever done, acquired, or experienced before. *This* is the unbelievable bond a woman cannot fathom before childbirth. *This* is the unexpected paradox of mothering: *we* are changed by the experience!

Being Transformed

Alexandra Stoddard in her book *Mothers* confirms and expands my experience by saying that "motherhood transforms us, not once, but over and over again."[1] Susan Maushart shares the following in her book, *The Mask of Motherhood:*

> For there are those (in plenty, the evidence suggests) for whom motherhood *is* experienced as all-fulfilling—those who, after the birth of a child, find their professional and social ambitions dwindling into disorienting indifference. They were led to anticipate motherhood as simply another of life's interesting options, and what they got instead was a full-scale transformation in values, identity, and lifestyle.[2]

Madonna, regardless of what you think of her lifestyle, has been transformed by motherhood. Rosie O'Donnell, Emmy-winning talk show host and single mother of three adopted children, redirected and transformed.[3] TV anchorwoman and mother of four, Maria Shriver, transformed.[4] Radio talk show host and mother of one, Dr. Laura Schlessinger, transformed.[5] For each of these women, and many others not in the public eye, the birth or adoption of a child marked not only the end of a period of waiting, but also the birth of a new kind of being—a mother.

Anne Roiphe, a writer active in more than three decades of the women's movement, writes in her late-in-life tribute to motherhood titled *Fruitful:*

> This [motherhood] was the beginning of my feminism and I don't care that that was an odd way to find it, a weird way to express it. I think many women know that their motherhood was the beginning of their

determination to stand strong against the currents that would take them away.[6]

I came to my own "feminism" through the same experience as Roiphe: through my children for whom I would stand against any storm. Motherhood transformed me as it did Stoddard, Maushart, Madonna, O'Donnell, Shriver, and Schlessinger. Motherhood gave me focus, direction, inner passion, and resolve—the intensity of which sometimes frightens me. In short, motherhood is nothing like I expected it to be.

For me, the currents that Roiphe spoke about, those that would take me away from my children, are the forces of our day and age that would seek to physically, mentally, emotionally, even spiritually separate me from them by telling me that pursuing a career is a better use of my life than mothering.

In an era of unprecedented freedom for women ushered in on the backs of many courageous pioneers, it has become expected that women, even when they become mothers, if not especially when they become mothers, should choose commitment to self and career over commitment to marriage and motherhood. Women who actively respond to the transformation that motherhood works in their lives are too often marginalized at work for choosing the "mommy track," or for choosing to consolidate their lives, quit work altogether, and focus unfragmented attention on home and family. Instead of being commended, they are branded with being "just a mom."

Why? Where do those expectations come from? Are they true? And why are our self-esteem, identity, and happiness so dependent on them? I propose that these expectations come primarily from three intertwined sources: (1) the popular media, (2) our peers, and (3) our mothers, and the feminists of their generation.

The Popular Media

For my generation of mothers and for me, the anti-mothering messages in the popular media are brutal. Women's magazines, politicians, even TV sitcoms entice us in word and image to put ourselves first, to become self-actualized above all else, and not to let marriage or motherhood get in our way. The media blares that we modern mothers, liberated from housework and childcare, should go for it—be free! We are told that we should expect to have it all and have it all right now. To the degree that we don't have it all, we should work longer hours so that we can pay more experts to raise our children and to tend to our homes so that we can go out and get it all.

Daily I battle the portrayal of a "perfect" mother such as the one shown on vacation in a recent TV advertisement. Sexy, in size eight stone-washed jeans, she gaily laughs into her cell phone while her two, perfectly groomed children (one boy and one girl) happily play at a soft-focus distance from her (not clinging to her leg like my children do when I am on the phone). Still on the phone, she flirts with a rakishly handsome man (who may or may not be her husband or the kids' father) who is grilling some fabulously expensive steaks next to the pool. (My husband is that handsome, but our steaks are of the ground variety and I am not flirting with anyone during the piranha hours between five and eight P.M.!) The media tells me that I *should* be able to have children *and* still have the figure of a sixteen-year-old model, *and* afford steak and luxury vacations, *and* capture and keep romance, *and* do it all with a smile on my face and perfect hair.

As a professional photographer, I am keenly aware that the media, especially through photography, has the power to typecast our expectations of the "good life." As the contemporary herald of our cultural expectations, the media is the first, most unrestricted, unquestioned saboteur of the ability to establish accurate and godly expectations for motherhood.

Who wouldn't want to look like the mom in that cell phone ad? Be on vacation with our kids like she is? Enjoy romance, laughter, and good food like she is? We never stop to realize that it is a setup. The expectation is false. The "mom" probably *is* sixteen years old. She is definitely acting on a set with complete strangers who are getting paid big bucks to look like her family and to make me feel inadequate and insecure as a mother so that I will buy the cell phone being advertised.

Narration for the PBS special, "American Photography; A Century of Images," politely lays bare the insidious media spawning these expectations by informing its viewers that "today [filmed in the late twentieth century] we buy as true and normal the Calvin Klein ad of a healthy, slim, sexy mother on the beach with two happy, clean kids."[7]

Unfortunately, the commentary continues, this image of motherhood is not any more true or normal than the "tightly defined" vision of motherhood presented in the 1950s TV ads depicting a middle-class, white, domesticated, mother-at-home with nothing more to worry over than her children's stained clothing or how to make the perfect pork chop. The narrator informs viewers that advertising and fashion photography show us the way we "wished" we looked; the way we "wished" we were, not the way we really are,[8] and yet we buy the expectation and are bitterly disappointed and disillusioned when it proves to be false. While the thoughts and feelings we encounter through exposure to the popular media are all real, they are produced by untruths.

Peer Expectations

The expectations of our peer groups (our girlfriends, our spouses, our sisters, our relatives) can stifle, suffocate, even strangle the profoundly unexpected joy motherhood brings into our lives. Husbands can be threatened by the turn of our affections to our children—even though they are their children, too. Girlfriends without children can also be threatened by the same turn of our hearts. Husbands vie for the return of romantic encounters. Girlfriends vie for the return of girls' night out and we ourselves vie for five minutes, just five minutes, of time alone without any relationship demands placed on our time or energy.

Most pressing among peer expectations is a spouse's expectation that a wife would remain in the work force, sharing the economic strain of raising the children. Many husbands of Generation X and younger have come to expect that we women would continue to "pull our financial weight" even after children arrive. Many wives continue with the same unrealistic expectation despite a new, inner voice that screams out against leaving a six-week-old infant in the hands of an unknown caregiver. Many of us do not even recognize that new, inner voice of a mother as being our own.

It's not that the economic strain isn't real. It is. Many couples purchase houses and cars based on joint incomes. Then, when the children (for whom the house and car were supposedly purchased) arrive, the big, beautiful new house in the suburbs stands empty for ten to twelve hours a day as mom, dad, and kids shuttle between work and daycare in order to keep up with the mortgage payments. And the moms look around at all their peers who are doing the same thing and think, "This must be how things are supposed to be, but this is not how I expected to feel."

On the other side, of course, are the mothers who choose to sacrifice their careers to be with their children and end up isolated in the house with crying babies all day. These moms look around at their peers and think, "This must be how things are supposed to be, but this is not how I expected to feel."

Many of the expectations of what mothering will be like that we assume from our peers are misleading at best. We've, none of us, been down this parenting road before. We do not have the same spouses, incomes, in-laws, education, numbers or personalities of children, housing options, or schooling options. That is not to say we can't enjoy real friendships with peers, but we should not expect to mother in the same way as our peers mother, even if to all appearances our situations in life are the same.

Our Mothers and the Feminist Generation

Many of our own mothers expected us to realize all the ambitions they never could; this clouds our ability to form realistic expectations of our own motherhood. Danielle Crittenden, author of *What Our Mothers Didn't Tell Us: Why Happiness Eludes the Modern Woman*, said in a radio interview that she believes the issues of feminism today are increasingly being debated between the generations rather than between the genders.[9] She corroborates this in her book:

> It's common now for the elders of the women's movement to express disappointment in my generation of women—the "daughters of the revolution" now in their twenties and thirties—who came of age long after the last feminist brassiere had been burned. As they see it, we are enjoying the spoils of their victories without any gratitude for their struggles.[10]

Crittenden encapsulates the message our generation has received from our mothers as "Do something with your life; don't depend on a man to take care of you; don't make the same mistakes I did." Dr. Laura Schlessinger echoes Crittenden's message, in her book *Parenting by Proxy*, by saying "she [her mother] frequently admonished me about how marriage, and especially children, inhibit a woman's happiness and enterprise."[11] Crittenden goes on to expose the profound error of the daughters who followed this advice given by a different generation:

So they [the daughters] have made different mistakes. They are women who postponed marriage and childbirth to pursue their careers only to find themselves at thirty-five still single and baby-crazy, with no husband in sight. Above all, these women are the majority of us, women who are hoping to do everything—work, children, marriage—only to ask ourselves why the pieces haven't added up the way we'd like or why we are collapsing under the strain of it all and doing everything badly.[12]

Despite our mothers' generation having advanced us daughters of the feminist revolution to the status of human beings, Crittenden points out that this advancement has not brought us happiness. It has brought us stress. We are faced with questions and potential answers that our mothers never faced. If they fought for the right to choose to engage in life outside of the home, we are fighting for the validity of the choice to remain engaged in life inside of the home. We wonder why it was okay, even valiant for them to choose to leave home and to enter the workplace, but is it not okay for us to choose to reenter the home? That's not really a matter of choice.

We fear that our mothers don't love our children, their grandchildren, because of their reaction to our choice to mother full time. There is the lingering ache that perhaps their misery was and is our fault. Perhaps, even, that they didn't love us when we were children—so that's why they either left us for the workplace or unceasingly grumbled about not leaving—like Schlessinger's mom—to the point of poisoning the idea of motherhood for us. Anne Roiphe writes that her daughter is "a critic of the [feminist] revolution in which I was a foot soldier," but to her credit, Roiphe does not begrudge her daughter the benefit of her revolutionary work, nor her daughter's right to question it.[13]

Our moms have been there, done that, in terms of raising children. They raised us and can often provide a lot of great guidance. But don't expect that everything your mom advises will, without a doubt, work for you. Intending no disrespect, question your mother's mothering advice. Take into full and honest account the situations surrounding her motherhood, and the influence that formed her expectations of it, before you let her views automatically color yours.

Why do these three intertwined sources of expectations— those of the popular media, of our peers, and of our mothers' generation of feminists—hold so much power over us? Why do we feel under siege and riddled with guilt, no matter how we fabricate our lives as mothers? I propose that it is because we have internalized these entangled expectations to the point of not even knowing that they are the enemy we are facing, not the people who are espousing them or the media that is imposing them. Trying to assess their individual influence is like trying to transplant a Morning Glory vine after it has already begun to wind its way up a trellis. Where does one interwoven coil of the plant begin and another end? Where does one begin to disconnect the parts so as not to destroy the whole?

Today as I write, after thirty-five "mother years" of experience (add your children's ages to calculate your own "mother years"), I can honestly tell you that none of my expectations of motherhood, those I assumed to be my own, those imposed on or offered to me by the media, by my peers, or by feminists from generations past, offered me or my children happiness or peace. Motherhood was not and is not anything like I expected it to be. It is more difficult. It is better. It is not tidy or capable of being organized. It is chaos and peace back-to-back.

Truly I went through the unexpected, full-scale transformation Stoddard and Maushart talk about. Today it is my children's interests that reignite my own, their child's-eye view of life that refreshes my pragmatic, grown-up perspective. And the more I look around, the more I see that I am not alone in experiencing this unexpected transformation, which caught me off guard and causes me to struggle to make the right choices, based on this new woman I've become. Motherhood has challenged the identity and self-worth of even the most accomplished and confident women I know. Perhaps, even, the more confident a woman beforehand, the more confounded afterward.

Having grown up in the shadow of the feminist movement, I expected to "be" something when I grew up. I expected to have, to do, and to be more than the "just-a-mom" that the media disparaged, that my not-yet-with-children peers snickered at, and that my own mother warned me against. The thought of being "just-a-mom" haunted me and threatened to crush whatever was left of my identity and self-worth after I had given birth. In her book *Ten Things I Wish I'd Known—Before I Went Out Into the Real World*, Maria Shriver recalls similar feelings of anxiety after giving birth to her first child.

> I held onto my unrealistic expectations [of seamlessly combining work and family] with both fists, spending most of my maternity leave trying to figure out exactly how I was going to manage this child and the travel and the job. I just knew I'd be able to figure it out, but as I looked around me for guidance and paths to follow, I found none. And where were the role models?[14]

I, too, looked for role models and found very few. So I began to devour books. Self-help and how-to books became my lifeline to unraveling what was, to me, the pivotal question: "What is the balance between who God made me to be as an individual, and the responsibilities God has given me as a mother?" In one of these books, *Works of Love are Works of Peace* by Michael Collopy, Mother Teresa of Calcutta is quoted as saying:

> We [the Missionaries of Charity] did not come to be social workers, but to belong to Jesus. Pray with Jesus and Jesus will pray with you.

Wherever God has put you, that is your vocation. It is not what we do but how much love we put into it. Where does love begin? It begins at home. Let us learn to love our family. In our own family we may have very poor people, and we do not notice them. We have no time to smile, no time to talk to each other. Let us bring that love, that tenderness into our own home and you will see the difference.[15]

Mother Teresa was not looking for a way to use her gifts and talents; she was looking to share the love of Jesus and ended up on the streets of Calcutta caring for the poor and the dying. She was not looking to strike a balance between what she did for herself and what she did for others; she was looking to serve the Lord.

Her message was that if God has given you a child, then you already have a job, a mission field, a purpose, a commission. According to this new perspective, motherhood—at its best—is the most worthwhile way for me to use not just some, but all of my gifts and talents. Motherhood, in and of itself, holds unlimited potential for self-expression. Not, mind you, the type of self-expression that the media, our peers, or our mothers' generation expects us to pursue, but the sort that God expects us to pursue; loving to our fullest potential.

My soul was unbound. In an instant, God pruned all my intercoiled, misguided expectations and transplanted a new and fuller understanding of motherhood in my heart. Truth was unveiled. My battle-weary heart rejoiced. In the saintly life of a nun, an unmarried woman who never bore a child of her own, I found a role model for motherhood.

The answer to my struggle with the disparate expectations of me as a woman, and then of me as a mother, was revealed not in perfecting some grand balancing act of these expectations, but in prioritizing their significance from a heavenly perspective. God is not nearly as impressed with my gifts and talents as I am. God is not as caught up in figuring out the best possible way to use me as I am.

And, I suspect, the same is true of God's perspective of the use of the collective gifts and talents of all humankind!

What God expects of us, first and foremost, is to respond to love by loving. It is what he has always expected because it is he who first loved us (1 John 4:19). God expects us to lovingly form and disciple our children. God expects us to present life to our children in such a way as to lead them to the saving love of Christ, no matter what other great opportunities to use our gifts and talents we are given and that we will have to learn to prioritize along the way.

"My husband was deployed for six weeks at sea when our first child was just two weeks old," recalls Diane, now a mother of four children. "That same day my mother returned to her home [5,000 miles away] after helping me. Watching my mom board that plane, leaving the baby and me alone and crying, I really realized that this was the start of my being the rock for the family. The make-up of my husband's job was just such that he could not be there all the time. And, being a teacher for five years before we had children [near the military base], I saw situations where kids were seriously affected by so much change and instability. Many kids suffered the fall-out of their home life being so unsettled. I just absolutely didn't want that for my children, so I couldn't keep a full-time job anymore. I had to be the constant. I just had to be.

"I was very aware of how out of step my choice was. But the out-of-step feeling wasn't enough to make me do anything differently. I liked what I was doing (being a mom) and I felt that there was no one doing this job better than I was."

We as a society have strayed so far from this simple, essential message about which Diane shares; it is a message of responding to the situations in which we find ourselves with as much love as possible. I now understand that I had woven into motherhood expectations of success, of self-satisfaction, and of "amounting to something" that had nothing to do with life and love. In fact, I had been taught that to love and take care of anyone in addition to myself was to be oppressed by him or her! Crittenden puts it plainly:

> For more than thirty years the women's movement has told us that we would be happier, more fulfilled human beings if we left our homes and went out to work. To the degree that we might feel misgivings or guilt about leaving our babies to others to raise we have been assured that such feelings are imposed upon us by society, and sexist—no more normal for a mother to experience than a father. Instead, we've been taught to suppress these worries and to put our work ahead of our families, or at the very least, to attempt to "balance" the demands of boss and baby. Any strong maternal feeling, any desire to surrender pieces of our professional selves, is viewed as reversion to some stereotype of motherhood the women's movement was supposed to have emancipated us from.[16]

Truly, it is not surprising that we, the "daughters of the revolution" are confused and confounded when we have children. Karen, mother of a six-month-old son, explained, "I expected to work my tail off in a job (motherhood) in which I had to keep reminding myself of the big picture to stay motivated and happy. This expectation was not met. I found motherhood to be hard work but with its rewarding moments every time I turn around (at least so far). I had anticipated motherhood to be much harder and less rewarding than is has turned out to be.

The expectations that many of us "daughters" have internalized of what will bring us peace and happiness have been sadly distorted. However, if we can lift the veil of unrealistic and inaccurate expectations, can we hope to rid our mothering souls of their influence? Yes. I believe we can if we will learn how to bear fruit. There are at least two biblical analogies of what we can expect life to be like. One is that of running a race. The other is of tending a vineyard (or a garden). If we apply the race analogy to motherhood, the basic idea is just this; don't expect to sprint to the finish line. "Life is a marathon," writes Maria Shriver, quoting her mother. "You can have and be all the things you want to be. Just do it over a lifetime. Don't try to do them all at once, because you can't. If you try to, everyone around you will suffer—mostly you."[17]

By applying the biblical analogy of tending a garden to motherhood, however, I think we are given a more generous understanding of the lifetime process. That is, considering all the experiences we will encounter as mothers, I think that it is accurate to expect that raising a child will be more like a ripening and less like a finish line.

Our worth, our abilities, cannot be summed up by having crossed a finish line, be it having met a deadline, or broken a glass ceiling, or delivered a baby. We do not fail but triumph when we allow motherhood to transform us from self-focused beings into other-focused, loving beings. We succeed in getting our priorities straight. When we bear fruit, the fruit of our wombs, we strive not for a finish line but for harvest time. Jesus speaks to the glory of this commissioning in the Gospel of John (15:8, 18): "It is to my Father's glory that you bear much fruit, showing yourselves to be my disciples…You did not choose me, but I chose you and appointed you to go and bear fruit—fruit that will last."

Whether we have children or not, God expects us to be fruitful, to use our gifts and talents to his glory. Without ever having children, Mother Teresa lived a fruitful life. But, because I *do* have children, God expects me to be fruitful in terms of mothering them with responsible love not comingled with selfish desires of my own career path or pursuits of temporal, personal happiness. God chose me to mother these specific children. He chose me to tend to them, to water them, to feed them, and in doing so to glorify God. God expects me to love my children—the fruit of my womb. There is no other point to be understood or responsibility to be balanced; love comes first.

Visualizing motherhood as something that will be done in seasons—planting, tending, and harvesting—helps us to loosen the unrealistic expectations that have bound us up. In order to visualize motherhood in this way, I carry with me an image of my children as seedlings planted in window boxes in late March while cold winds still chill the air and the ground outside remains frozen below the melting snow. The little lime-green shoots that soon poke up through the nutrient-rich black soil and strain toward the sun in the window are not yet ready to be planted in the garden; the time is not right. But she who planted them continues to sustain them through April with watering and a place near the window until the warmth of May or even June has come, and the partially grown sprouts are hardy enough to be planted outdoors.

We will not always have toddlers underfoot needing our constant attention as do window boxes in March. Neither will we always have teenagers hanging around, growing as rapidly and in every direction as bean sprouts in July. But each day of each season, we will have the opportunity to love. And, if we faithfully tend our children as seedlings, "then our sons (and daughters) in their youth will be like well-nurtured plants," David proclaims in Psalm 144:12. Here is the truth. In every season, our garden will reflect the care—the love—we have given to it.

Motherhood may not always be what we expected it to be. But, when we make our family members or ourselves the focal point of our disappointments, rather than the realities of life that did not meet our preconceived expectations (as I did when I thought I had "failed" to get up and run around the cranberry bogs), our anger is unjust, misplaced, and unproductive. If we do not periodically readjust our expectations to reflect reality, we will do long-term damage to ourselves and to our entire family. We will bear sour fruit, mealy fruit, or no fruit at all.

To mothers, like myself, who want to make some changes in their mothering styles so they can tend their seedlings more lovingly,

Mother Teresa gives wise council from her experience of giving aid to the poor:

> I never look at the masses as my responsibility. I look only at the individual. I can love only one person at a time. I can feed only one person at a time. Just one, one, one. Same thing for you. Same thing in your family. Same thing in the church where you go. Just begin…one, one, one. At the end of our lives, we will not be judged by how many diplomas we have received, how much money we have made or how many great things we have done. We will be judged by "I was hungry and you gave me to eat. I was naked and you clothed me. I was homeless and you took me in."[18] (Scripture paraphrased by Mother Teresa from Matthew 25:31–46.)

If you are a mother, expect to love and to be loved. If you have planted children in your home, expect to use all of your gifts and talents in keeping up with them—watering, weeding, and harvesting. Live life in its season. Learn to expect the unexpected and to embrace new expectations. It will bring you peace.

Focus Questions for Making Peace

1. List three or more expectations you have for your motherhood. List at least one from each area.

Media/cultural expectations:

Peer expectations:

Expectations from your mother's generation of women:

2. Think about the things you listed above and then explain why these expectations might be simply unrealistic or ungodly for you in this season of motherhood.

Media/cultural expectations:

Peer expectations:

Expectations from your mother's generation of women:

3. Read John 15. How does it feel to know that God has chosen you, appointed you to bear fruit in the form of children?

4. Choose one simply unrealistic or ungodly expectation that you have of motherhood that you would like to change. Pray now and daily for the guidance of the Holy Spirit in helping you to change that expectation. Write down here one concrete way to begin doing so today.

Chapter 2

Gifted Mothering: Identity and Self-Worth

In the middle of packing a picnic lunch for our family of six (at that time), I sneaked a quick phone call to my mom. As the peanut butter flew off my knife and a whole loaf of bread stacked up into sandwiches, I shared with her our plans to enjoy a Sunday at the beach as a family. During our conversation I casually asked her, "So, what are you and Dad up to today?"

Stammering at first, my mom quickly launched into a long list of impressive-sounding, important activities that she and my dad had lined up for the day—a Sunday. I was taken aback until I realized that instead of asking her a simple question, I had unintentionally issued her a threat. "Prove to me how worthy you are by listing how many important things you are doing," is what she heard me say. Like so many other mothers, including myself, my mother was put on the defensive by my question, even though none of her kids live at home any longer. And do you know what? Often it is exactly that same threat to my identity and self-worth that I hear when my husband returns home from work and innocently says, "Hi, honey. What did you do today?" Most days when he waltzes through the door I am up to my elbows in dishes and whining kids, half of the supper is still frozen and the other half is about to burn, there are piles of laundry cascading down my couch in which a child or two is playing hide-and-seek, and I am in no mood for polite conversation. "What did I do today?!" I growl at him.

Because I work out of my house, I once unknowingly answered a phone call from my editor in the middle of changing a diaper. All of a sudden, I found myself trying to balance the phone on my shoulder, finish the job on my squirming, screaming baby, and sound convincingly professional all at the same time. (Very soon after that balancing act, I ordered a separate business line with its own message center!)

My editor's completely innocent request was, "Can you fax me a summary of who you are—you know, just a quick bio? We need one for the new catalog—today." "You know what," I unprofessionally sighed into the phone, at the same time releasing the freshly diaper-clad baby, "I don't really want all those people to know who I am! How about just including a photograph and letting them guess the rest by the bags under my eyes?"

Identity and self-worth. For several years I have been giving a presentation about these two elusive concepts to women's groups, which I titled "I am a Gift from God." My goal in giving these presentations is to help women clarify the proper source of their identity and self-worth. The message is targeted toward women who, in becoming mothers, may have lost their sense of self.

Potential Periods of Identity Crises

The first thing I discovered, when talking with a diverse cross-section of mothers while developing the "Gift" presentation, was that not only did almost every woman experience various identity crises upon becoming a mother, but that there was a pattern to these crises. The pattern that emerged included three predictable crisis periods:

(1) *Birth and New Baby:* The first potential identity crisis of motherhood takes place when the first baby arrives and active mothering begins. This is a period of huge adjustment including, for some,

the loss of individual identity and income wrapped up in a career left behind. For others, this crisis period includes adjusting to the influences of daycare and absentee parenting.

(2) *Off to Kindergarten:* The second potential identity crisis comes when each child hops on the school bus and is off to kindergarten. If it is the youngest child, the house is suddenly very, very quiet after many loud and boisterous preschool years. Even if a mother educates her children at home, the very act of beginning a formal school program signals a fundamental change in the household routine and the mother's identity in relation to her child.

(3) *Leaving the Nest:* The third potential identity crisis begins when each child hops in that car or on that plane and leaves the nest—perhaps off to college, or to a new apartment or house of their own. If it is the youngest child, all of a sudden there is no longer a game or school meeting to get to, or any other pressing reason to hurry through dinner. Active mothering draws to a close.

All mothers go through these three periods of potential identity crisis in the natural progression of motherhood. They are universal parts of the seasons of motherhood and they strain even the healthiest marriages. There are, of course, other situations that will be occasions for an identity crisis such as the loss or serious illness of a child, a spouse, or a close family member; moving to a new town; a grown child's moving back home; or maybe becoming a mother-in-law and a grandmother.

How mothers get through, or do not get through, these periods depends largely on the source of their identity and self-worth. As a part of the "I am a Gift from God" program, I ask the women in the audience to answer three very basic questions: "Who are you?" "How do you know who you are?" and "What do you do?"

Let me describe five of the categories of answers I have received from the hundreds of mothers surveyed. Most of the women I surveyed were Christian women, actively involved in their faith communities. Their answers reveal the sources from which we as mothers are attempting to draw our identities and why the sources are not providing the security and the value we need to be confident and joyful in motherhood.

You will identify with one of the categories most strongly, but not exclusively. I distinguish the identity categories, not to pigeonhole you, but to help you understand your natural bent. Read each category so that at the end of the chapter you can embrace the sixth— the most godly, but perhaps most unnatural—identity that you have been given.

A Relationship Identity

A woman who has a relationship identity will answer the question "Who are you?" with a relationship: "I am a mother," or perhaps, "I am a wife." This is a relationship identity. When I ask how they know who they are, moms who identify themselves by relationships have said things like:

> "Because my kids are always yelling 'mom' this and 'mom' that. I hear it constantly."
> "Other people define me; I'm his wife, her mom, her daughter…."
> "Because being a caretaker is what I'm comfortable with."
> "Because taking care of my kids takes up most of my time."
> "I just feel it. I am connected to others."

With answers like these we may be trying to assume identity and value from relationships with other people.

An example of a relationship mom is one who cooks the perfect dinner of, say, oven-roasted chicken, steamed green beans, and mashed potatoes, only to have Junior say that he doesn't like the dinner, so she goes and fixes him an entirely new meal. It is more important to a relationship mom that the relationship between herself and her child is good than that the dinner is good.

A woman with a relationship identity is usually a very natural mother. She is loving, expressive with her affection, and willing to invest energy in her children. Motherhood, however, can completely overwhelm the relationship mom with its conflicting demands. She finds it impossible to satisfy the needs of all her relationships and to satisfy her own needs as well. While she is tending to one relationship, she feels guilty about not tending to another. A relationship mom usually puts the needs of others well ahead of her own, compounding her resentment about not having time for her own needs.

When it comes to the three potential periods of identity crisis, birth and new motherhood will be fairly easy for this mom; she welcomes the new relationship into her life. Off to kindergarten and leaving the nest—time for a crisis. "Empty-nest syndrome" hits hard for this woman, who has probably neglected to develop her own interests in the process of parenting. Having placed too much responsibility on her children to keep her happy, she may become an ace at putting guilt trips on the kids for "abandoning" her for jobs, spouses, and children of their own. A typical relationship mom usually invests too much of herself in her children, putting a great deal of stress on her marriage in doing so.

A Responsibility Identity

Another answer to "Who are you?" can be "I am an artist," or perhaps, "I am a systems analyst," or a job title of some sort indicating a responsibility identity. When I ask how they know who they are, responsibility moms have said things like:

"Who I am is what I spend my time doing."
"My past accomplishments tell me who I am."
"I pay my bills."

"I am defined by the responsibilities in my life."
"I know who I am because of all my effort."

With this type of answer we may be trying to earn identity and value through responsibilities. An example of a responsibility mom is one who cooks the perfect dinner of, say, oven-roasted chicken, steamed green beans, and mashed potatoes, only to have Junior say that he doesn't like the dinner, but she makes him eat it anyway (and drink all his milk).

It is more important to a responsibility mom that she is responsibly providing for the nutritional needs of her family than that her child like the dinner. This mom is not just making a meal, she is a chef! Liking the food is of secondary importance.

A woman with a responsibility identity is a natural at the *concept* of motherhood. She will read every book in the library on the topic. She will be organized and efficient in getting her child everything he needs. The initial transition into the birth and new baby period, however, may be difficult for this woman. Bonding with an infant is mostly about responding to the wonder of new life—pondering the beauty of this being *my* child and beginning to build a relationship that will sustain a lifetime of responsibilities. The actual act of mothering, as opposed to the concept of motherhood, may frustrate the responsibility-driven woman who thrives on goals and accomplishments. The goals of mothering are too long-term and the accomplishments are too intangible. Frankly, you cannot force a two-year-old child to be potty trained just because it is on your "To Do" list for the week!

Off to kindergarten and leaving the nest are comparatively easy for this mom; she welcomes the opportunity to get involved in the PTA or to add a second income to the family to help pay for college. She can *do* these things. The responsibility mom usually does not invest enough of herself in her children and her marriage. She is concerned with doing, not being. She would prefer to sit on a committee than to sit with her child. This mom often forgets the value of long hugs and tender kisses.

A Self-Reliant Identity

Women for whom neither relationships nor responsibilities have brought positive self-worth will answer "Who are you?" with a simple "I am me." No last name, no associations; me, plain and simple, take it or leave it. This is a self-reliant identity. When I ask them how they know who they are, self-reliant moms have said things like:

"It's been 41 years!"
"I choose to be who I am."
"I don't know. No clue."
"Um, didn't I just tell you my name?"
"What do you mean? Do you want me to look in the
     mirror, or something?"

A self-reliant mom's answer is often marked with individualism. Frequently it is tinged with anger as well, followed by a suspicious, "Why are you asking? What do you care?" An example of a self-reliant mom is a woman who when confronted with the need to provide dinner for her children responds by thinking, if not actually saying, "Dinner? Last time I checked there was food in the kitchen....Do I look like the hired help around here?" This woman knows that neither an identity based on relationships nor on responsibilities completely satisfies. She has tried them both and neither one worked.

All three potential identity crisis periods will be tough for a self-reliant mom: birth and new baby, off to kindergarten, and leaving the nest. A woman with a self-reliant identity is a natural at leadership. She is capable of handling just about anything. However, while she may give the impression of being independent and tough, it is a good front. The self-reliant mother is often quite lonely for a number of reasons. She is more fragile than she appears and is most likely hurting inside. The self-reliant mom responds to disappointing relationships and unrewarding responsibilities by getting a thick skin, a hardened heart, and possibly a divorce before the age of thirty.

The first three categories of answers—from relationship moms, responsibility moms, and self-reliant moms—demonstrate our human need for identity and value. Most of us want to have safe, supportive relationships. We want to use our talents and to grow in our job responsibilities. We want to be free to express ourselves. These are normal and healthy desires. Relationships and responsibilities are not bad. In their place they are vital, wonderful parts of our lives. We should continue to develop our lives in all three areas, but we must not let ourselves be defined by who we are related to, what we do with our time, nor by past frustrations or failures in either area. Why not? Because these things will change again and again over our lifetimes, just as they did when the first child arrived. This is very important to understand.

As mothers we need positive self-esteem that is not measured by how many subordinates we supervise and how much money we make, nor by how many children we have and how much money we save! Motherhood is not like anything we have ever done before. Motherhood is a ministry. It is a ministry about love. It is not about accounting for numbers of dollars made or saved or for numbers of kids or promotions gained or lost. Motherhood is more than a job. It is more than just managing the monster, I mean the child we've created. God himself calls us to motherhood. Our motherhood will be as unique as we are.

The truth of this is complicated by the American media culture that is eager to provide for us the fourth identity—the mythical, ideal Super-Mom identity, against which we mortal moms feel obliged to compare ourselves.

Super-Mom Identity

An example of a woman with a Super-Mom identity is a mom who has great plans of family time spent around the dinner table, but has taken the kids to McDonald's more times than she can count because she is always carpooling around dinnertime. Oven-roasted chicken, steamed beans, and mashed potatoes are figments of this mother's imagination. Stress is her mantra as she tries to be all three of the mothers we just discussed combined into one. Birth and new baby, off to kindergarten, and off to college will all be stressful for this mom because she has bought the lie that she can have it all, all of the time, but she just can't figure out why it seems to work for everyone but her.

The hidden kicker about the Super-Mom identity is that I think that most of us know someone who we think is, in fact, Super-Mom dressed in plain clothes. Kathleen's story is an example of how ridiculous it can get when we compete to be the "super-est" mom out there. Kathleen has six children aged eighteen to three and is expecting her seventh in five months. Even if we stopped right there, this woman, to me, could already be considered "Super-Mom." She also home schools all the children because her husband is in the military and they move every few years. She and her family currently live overseas, where they have been stationed for the past four years. On top of these extraordinary mothering responsibilities, she is currently leading a women's prayer group, cofacilitating a church youth group for military teenagers, and heading up a new, international support group for mothering. Recently she phoned and told me that her husband would be retiring from the military and looking for a civilian job back in the United States.

As I listened to my friend, I began to count the enormous adjustments she'd be making in the next six months: giving birth to her seventh child, sending her first child off to college, moving her family back to some currently unknown place in the United States after four years overseas, and losing the twenty-one-year-long security of her husband's military job. All this added up to what I considered an already heavy load of caring for and schooling six, soon-to-be seven, children and keeping the house in any sort of order. I promised to pray for her before we hung up.

A short time after we talked I received an e-mail from her saying that the homeschooling organization with which she was affiliated had just asked her to become a consultant to other moms registered with the organization. Her response? "I told them that I thought, perhaps, when I was settled next year I would consider it for the following year. It was funny, though, because I know many women who would attempt it despite the arrival of a new baby, change of job, moving, et cetera. I must fight the urge to leap tall buildings."

I was flabbergasted. Even a mom whom most of us mere mortal moms would have perceived as doing everything plus, then even a little more, felt the need to compare herself to some even more super Super-Mom. We've got to send Super-Mom back to her own planet.

An Object Identity

A woman with an object identity finds most of her self-worth wrapped up in a coveted object: a beautiful home in the right neighborhood, the most sought-after SUV, the most fashionable haircut or wardrobe. In some cases children are coveted as objects of prestige, increasing or decreasing a mother's value or social status by their performances. This is not the same as a relationship identity, where the relationship with, not the performance of, a child is the basis of a mother's identity.

None of the women I've interviewed have ever answered the "Who are you?" question with the name of an object or a thing. My question is not worded in a way that they really could. However, an object identity can be worn in tandem with any one of the previous four identities and it is not hard to detect having one if you are really honest with yourself. The easiest way to discover if you have an object identity is to lose that object: to have to sell your home and move into a smaller one in a less desirable neighborhood, to crash your car and have to drive the rental car that the insurance company provides, or to show up at church just after camping or traveling and not have time to primp and preen. Again, objects are not bad. Wanting to be comfortable in your car and in your clothes is not bad. They are natural desires, but at what price? Having an unhealthy need or identification with our possessions can lead us to make poor mothering choices. Having an object identity can cause us to keep an object, say an expensive car, in order to maintain our identity when, in fact, our family finances would be infinitely better off with a less expensive vehicle.

So here then is the essential question: How is it possible to have an identity apart from our relationships, how we spend our time, and what we possess? If relationships, responsibilities, and objects are not bad, but shouldn't provide all of our identity and self-worth, from where should we as mothers draw these things? It is really quite a plot twist. On one hand mothers are invaluable. Jobs are important. Objects are necessary. And it is natural and good to want to be the best or to have the best of each of these things. On the other hand, if we make any of them the object of our desire, the foundation of our identity and self-worth, we destroy their goodness. Where do we begin to work loose such an entangled knot?

We begin with knowing Jesus. In order to untie identity and self-worth from our relationships, responsibilities, and objects, we must know who we are in Christ. We must know that God's will and God's call are two different things.

God's Will

God's *will* is that we know him, love him, and serve him. God's *will* is summed up in all the commandments and the directives we find written in the Bible. His *will* is unchanging, always the same for every person. It is in his *will* that we find our identity in being his child.

We are actually given names in the Bible with which we can answer that question "Who are you?" Some of my favorites are that we are God's precious children (Eph 1:15), which means that we are daughters of the King of Kings (Ps 45:9). We are princesses! We are the jewels in the Father's crown (Zech 9:16). And my personal favorite: We are gifts from God to Jesus (John 17:6, 24).

A Gift Identity

With this "Gift Identity" we receive our indisputable self-worth. God loves us and created us as very special gifts for Jesus. No person, position, place, or possession can change this identity. Because of our Gift Identity we do not have to adopt self-reliant identities when relationships fail or responsibilities overwhelm. We can accept change and move on. We do not have to aspire to be Super-Mom and do it all. We can let someone else run the Christmas Bazaar this year. We can postpone the purchase of a home, stop working altogether, postpone girls' night out, and generally clear our plates when we have children, by realizing that who we are in Christ is not affected by these external, temporal changes. When asked how they know who they are, moms with Christ-centered Gift Identities have said things like:

> "I know I am a child of God because the Bible tells me I am."

"My upbringing from my parents taught me that I am God's child."

"My relationship to Christ tells me who I am."

A mother is not who you are, but how you are related to your children. No single relationship adds up to a person's full identity. A job title, no matter what the rank or importance, is not who you are but a description of what you do. No single responsibility comes close to correctly identifying who a person is. If it could, every single doctor, teacher, or grocery store clerk you've ever met would have to be the same. But they are not, are they?

Because of Jesus' life, death, and resurrection, it does not matter how other people judge your worth and your work. Most important, nothing you or I can ever do, nor anyone we will ever know, can change our Gift Identity. Not birth and new baby. Not off to kindergarten. Not leaving the nest. Not losing or getting a job. Not buying or selling the house. Not even death or divorce can change your Gift Identity.

Many times it is the woman who is trying to do her best at mothering that ends up engaged in this almost frantic search for self, this trying on of all sorts of identities. Because her mothering goes so unnoticed and is so undervalued by society, this mom will volunteer for everything in sight just to gain any amount of recognition beyond her own four walls. A teenage friend, Samantha, confides that although her mother has never held a paying job, she is out of the house four and five evenings a week running between committee meetings, volunteering, attending a church activity, or setting off for various other important functions.

"I'm sure we eat dinner together some nights," says Samantha, trying to conjure up a specific memory, "but not very many. I definitely get the impression that my mom has more pressing things to do than to take care of the house or hang around with the family. It feels like she is always working overtime, but it isn't like she has a job or anything…it is kind of bizarre. Someone or something always needs her more than we do."

Kay has also witnessed this pattern of seeking approval and recognition to the detriment of family life. "I have this friend, Jane, who continually over-commits to the point that nothing she does ever gets done even halfway. Things pile up so badly that she quits whatever has gone awry, leaving everyone in the lurch. Because her husband is in the military and they do not live in one place for very long, Jane sees the next move as a huge release from all the messes she's created and yet moves somewhere else and does the exact same thing again. Does she stop and take note of the pattern? No! Her need for recognition is almost pathological. Her kids and husband are usually the main casualties. But I realize that it is that hunger for God that is really at the root of it all and that she will never get better if she doesn't draw all the recognition she needs from him." Kay's story puts the importance of knowing God's will in a nutshell. Until we are fixed firmly as individuals in God's unchanging love, we are like unanchored boats in a storm, hurled about at the whim of the waves and wind. We are unable to make *consistently* good choices about how and where God is calling us to spend our time, our energy, and our resources.

God's Call

Unlike God's will, God's *call* is special and unique to each of us as individuals. His specific call changes not only from woman to woman, but throughout each woman's life. Not every woman will be a mother. It is under the category of God's *call* that motherhood fits, not under his will. It is under the category of God's *call* that relationships, responsibilities, and objects fit. They are unique, special, individually designed, and not to be compared between mothers!

Some of them are going to work for you; others are not. Understanding the difference between God's *will* and God's *call* in our lives, we can as mothers begin to enjoy the relationships, responsibilities, and objects that energize us without them defining who we are and what we should do with our time. Better still, we can say no to those things that drag us down without having to feel like we've failed. Casting off the burdensome identities generated by relationships, responsibilities, and objects, we can focus on loving our children without demanding identity or reward for our efforts. Motherhood can become a delight that we share with our children, rather than a demand we shoulder as best we can. By accepting Jesus as your personal Lord and Savior you accept your Gift Identity. By rejecting the identities that come along with relationships, responsibilities, and objects, you begin to live your Gift Identity.

Psalm 127:3 tells us that children are a gift from the Lord. Can you envision God giving this beautiful gift box that is you to Jesus? Feel Jesus' loving embrace. Feel his strong and capable hands holding you. In the book of Isaiah (49:15–16) we read: "See! I will not forget you…I have carved you on the palm of my hand. I have called you by your name. You are mine. You are precious to me. I love you." God loves you.

Whether you have one child or fifteen, adopted or step, whether you work inside or outside of the home, part-time, full-time, or volunteer, God loves you. Responsibilities, relationships, and desirable objects will change again and again with the seasons of life; don't stake your identity and self-worth on them. Stake your identity on being created by God as a precious gift for his Son Jesus; this will never change.

Focus Questions for Making Peace

1. With which identity—relationship, responsibility, self-reliant, Super-Mom, or object—did you most identify? Why?

2. What are some of the positive and negative consequences of maintaining this identity?

3. Do you accept God's will for you—your Gift Identity? What are the helpful aspects of having a Gift Identity? What are the difficult aspects?

4. Read the following statements. Pick three of these, adapted from the Bible, that mean the most to you and tell why.

I am significant, acceptable, and secure because...

I am not "just" a mother. I am a gift from God to Jesus.

Jesus thanks his Father God for the gift of me (John 17:6, 24).

I am God's handiwork (Eph 2:10).

I am loved by God (Jer 31:3).

I am God's child (John 1:12; 1 John 3:1–3).

I have been redeemed and forgiven of all my sins (Col 1:14).

I am complete in Christ (Col 2:10).

I am confident that the good work that God has begun in me will be completed (Phil 1:6).

I am the salt of the earth (Matt 5:13).

I am the light of the world (Matt 5:14).

I am a branch of the true vine, a channel of his life (John 15:1, 5).

I am a personal witness for Christ (Acts 1:8).

I am God's temple (1 Cor 3:16).

I am a member of Christ's body (1 Cor 3:9; 2 Cor 12:27).

I am God's co-worker (1 Cor 3:9; 2 Cor 6:1).

I am a saint (Eph 1:1).

I am a citizen of heaven (Eph 2:6; Phil 3:20).

I am Christ's friend (John 15:15).

I am born of God (1 John 5:18).

I am never alone (Heb 13:5).

I cannot be separated from the love of God (Rom 8:35).

I have been chosen and appointed to bear fruit (John 15:16).

I have not been given a spirit of fear, but of power, love, and a sound mind (2 Tim 1:7).

I have direct access to God through the Holy Spirit (Eph 2:18).

(The above statements are adapted in part from Dr. Neil T. Anderson, *Steps to Freedom in Christ*.)

God wants me…

To share with my child the love he has for me. God promises that as I grow in love for him, he will give me more love for others (John 15:5; Rom 5:5; 1 John 4:9).

To love others as God has loved me (1 John 4:9).

To pray in the Spirit on all occasions with all kinds of prayers and requests (Eph 6:18).

To use the talents he has given me to produce good fruit (John 15:5).

To know that my labor in the Lord is not in vain (1 Cor 15:5).

To never fret (Ps 37:1).

To trust in the Lord and do good (Ps 37:3).

To do all in word or deed in the name of the Lord Jesus (Col 3:17).

To be still before the Lord and wait patiently for him (Ps 37:7).

To bless my family with the work of my hands (Prov 31:12–24).

To look after the needs of my household and not eat the bread of idleness (Prov 31:27).

To be quick to hear, slow to speak, and slow to anger (Jas 1:19).

To never worry about my life, what I will eat, or what I will wear (Luke 12:22).

To clothe myself with compassion, kindness, humility, gentleness, and patience (Col 3:12).

To obey what Jesus commands (John 14:15).

To control my tongue; that my speech may benefit those who listen (Eph 4:29).

To bring up my children in the training and instruction of the Lord (Eph 5:2).

To take care of my physical body (Eph 5:29).

To honor healthy sexuality in marriage (Heb 13:4).

To be fruitful and multiply (Gen 1:28).

To bear with others' faults and forgive whatever grievances I may have (Col 3:13; Gal 6:2).

To avoid foolish conversations, arguments, and quarrels (Titus 3:2, 9).

To warn those who are idle, to encourage the timid, to help the weak, to be patient (1 Thess 5:14).

To train younger women to love their families, to be self-controlled, and to be busy at home (Titus 2:3–5).

Chapter 3

Weaving Home and Work: Understanding Yourself

Recently I had the pleasure of being introduced by a new friend as "a woman who knows why she gets up in the morning...the most defined mother I have ever met." I say this was a pleasure because being described as "defined" or having a purpose worth getting up for was a new character trait for me. Brand new. When I began my life as a mother I was so unfocused and unsure of myself that my sister-in-law, Tami, jokingly dubbed me a "reluctant mother." And she was quite right.

In my struggle for peace about the purpose of motherhood and the duties that tagged along with that purpose, I was caught between two polarized caricatures—that of a housewife and that of a career woman. I had made a concrete choice to make our family, not a career, the focus of my creative energies, but I did *not* want to be a housewife. The Random House Dictionary defines a housewife as "the woman in charge of the household, especially a wife who does all or most of the cleaning and cooking in her own household and who holds no other job." It was not a definition I desired to fill! But, by holding no job outside the house, I supposed that by default a housewife is what I had to be, and I hated it. I hated the very idea of being a housewife so much that I dressed up the definition of my new duties with the title "Family Architect—Fabrication Division" in order not to put "housewife" as my occupation when filling out forms. My brother-in-law, Francis, even had business cards printed up for me with that job title on them—something we look back at and laugh about today.

Becoming a Home-Based, Family-Centered Mom

In the beginning I worked hard to domesticate myself. I tried diligently to drag my carefree, creative spirit indoors, and to find joy in household activities like cooking and cleaning, but it was so unnatural. For the sake of my children, I was willing to unnaturally stuff myself into the housewife box because I really wanted to be a good mother and thought that being at home was the best way to be one, but darned if my spirit didn't keep hopping out! It was as if I was the Wizard of Oz. My life was one of smoke and curtains as I pretended to love my new housebound, domestic life and give the appearance of being a good housefrau. Truthfully, I wasn't convinced of the importance or value of what I was doing. But my heart's desire to respond correctly to motherhood seemed to overrule my head, which was in a whirlwind of confusion. Again, I thought being at home was the best and the right thing to do for my kids, so I just did it even though it did not "feel" right at all.

In her book, *The Mask of Motherhood*, Susan Maushart calls "masks" the various roles women with children play and the issues they must choose to either address or avoid (such as working outside the home, bottle- or breast-feeding, childcare, housework, and the character of marriage after babies). Maushart says that these mother-masks are colored by a woman's satisfaction or dissatisfaction with her choices on these issues. Further stating that "all masks are props for pretending," Maushart proceeds throughout her book to decorate the masks of motherhood with the various anxieties that each one adds to a woman's life.[19] In his book, *What's So Amazing About Grace?* Philip Yancey talks about masks, too. He says that the word *hypocrisy* as Jesus used it in the Sermon on the Mount means "simply, 'putting on a mask.'" Yancey says that Jesus evidently coined the word, "borrowing it from the Greek actors, or hypocrites, who entertained crowds at an outdoor theater near his home. It describes a person who puts on a face to make a good impression."[20]

I would have never thought of myself as a hypocrite, but looking back, I was definitely putting on a face—wearing all those different masks of a happy housewife to hide my inner turmoil. I was intimately acquainted with the instinct to hide my true feelings in order to give a good impression. As I began to respond to the transformation that motherhood was working in my life and to pray and ask God to reveal his call on my life (his special plan for the relationships, responsibilities, and material things in my life), a new image of the various roles and duties I was juggling arose. It was the image of hats, not masks. I liked the hat image better than the mask image. While giving credit to the notion that these duties and roles are still props in one form or another (not really the essence of who we are in Christ), we do not *hide* behind hats. We dress ourselves up in them. We wear different hats for different seasons. Hats are both fun and functional. We can even wear more than one hat at the same time. But we do not hide behind them.

Connie Fourre Zimney gave me great perspective on the term *housewife* in her book, *In Praise of Homemaking*, when she said, "The tasks that fill my days are really done for the purpose of making our house a home for my family."[21] She recognized her role as mother as that of an artist—a person who takes raw materials and creates something "capable of making a statement and touching the heart."[22] In Zimney's case, she saw people, place, and time as the raw materials a woman/artist had the privilege of shaping into a home.

Zimney helped me to see that the concept of homemaking had been vandalized. The term *housewife* was a remnant of the original feminist movement that was trying to pinpoint the "problem that has no name"[23] and ended up developing the caricature of a pitiful creature named "housewife" who had been robbed of the joy of creating a home and had been enslaved to the drudgery of housekeeping. A woman named Jenny shares her surprise at experiencing the joy of homemaking.

> After going to a part-time schedule, I was shocked to enjoy getting home early enough to start dinner for my husband and daughter. I had never thought of typical "housewife" chores as rewarding; on the contrary, I thought I would resent having to do them. But it felt good to be there for my family instead of running through the door after they had been home and done eating for 30 minutes.[24]

Joy of joys! I wasn't a housewife just because I didn't have a career. There was a purpose to the mundane duties of caring for a house and children. The purpose was to create an environment where I could educate my children in the faith and point them to their eternal home in heaven. Perfection or even greatness in the day-to-day duties of housekeeping was not the point. The duties of maintaining a household merely provided the support system for the broader purpose of motherhood. But—and this was the big *but* that changed my life—without a strong, secure support system, the lofty purpose of motherhood would remain an elusive dream, a house of cards destined to collapse. "Let us not despise the day of small things nor grow weary in well-doing,"[25] says author and educator Susan Macaulay of the formation and discipline of young children, in her book *For the Children's Sake*.

Finally, comprehending this big *but*, I have pulled myself back from the extreme thinking that to maintain a household is drudgery, destining one to becoming a bored and boring housewife. Understanding the bigger purpose of creating a home brought my heart and head together. I now take great pleasure in designing organizational systems for meal planning, laundry, house cleaning,

Sabbath activities, and space use to maximize my mothering impact. I derive great joy from running my well-oiled home.

Larry Burkett estimated, in his book *Women Leaving the Workplace*, that "if only the direct financial value of her (mom's) services is calculated in terms of cleaning, cooking, sewing, delivering, and shopping, the net value totals about $20,000 a year (written in 1995)....[B]ut, you can't hire the caring, compassion, and devotion of a mother at any price. When was the last time you heard of a housekeeper who sat up all night with a sick child? There may be a few, but you can't hire them for $20,000 a year. The bottom line is, a mother is worth a lot more to her family than most employers can ever afford to pay."[26]

As it was accurately written in an e-mail forward I received called "Fun Quotes from Women," "the phrase 'working mother' is redundant!"[27] Mothering is work. So is running a household, a duty that often gets lumped into the same pot without adequate differentiation. Not only is mothering work, as Burkett demonstrated, it is work on which you could put an actual price tag if it helped you to do so. Furthermore, in calculating the price, you would discover that such personalized care is not affordable, not to mention the loving sacrifices a mother makes to provide it to her family. The work of mothering is priceless.

Being a Professional without Having a Career

As I continued to pray about God's call in my life, I also realized that my understanding of the opposite extreme of a housewife, a career woman, was also misguided if not downright wrong. Just as I had assumed homemaking to be masochistic self-sacrifice to pointless drudgery, I also assumed that pursuing any personal interests outside of mothering was hedonistic and a self-indulgent neglect of one's children. Not so.

Looking around at some of the best mothers I knew, I noticed that most of them, whom I had earlier assumed to be housewives, were passionately engaged both in mothering and in activities outside of mothering! At first this surprised me, or at least defied my expectations. As I got to know these women better, I discovered that the activities in which they were engaged could be grouped into four different categories: (1) volunteering in the community, (2) home-based businesses or part-time, flexible employment outside the home, (3) home-schooling, and (4) continuing education. These women were definitely not career women, keeping a job as their principal occupation, but they were definitely not housewives either, cooking and cleaning all day. As I took a closer look, I could see that each mom had taken care to put the needs of her family first. Each had excellent organizational skills. Each recognized the important work of creating a loving home environment, in part by cooking meals and keeping the house clean. Each cared for her children personally or with as little use of daycare as possible. Each had a passion both for mothering *and* for the activities in which she was involved outside of mothering. These women neither belittled nor exalted mothering, nor their outside activities. Each simply, carefully, and consistently chose to put the needs of her family first. Without being tied to a specific career, each was a shining example of a professional as defined by Webster's Dictionary as "a person who is expert at his or her work."

Jill Savage is one of these shining examples. As the mother of four children, she took the professional approach to mothering and ran with it. After learning to be an "expert mom" in her own home, Jill felt God's call to encourage other moms who wanted to do the same. The result was the founding of the Hearts at Home ministry, which conducts one-day "professional" conferences for over 15,000 women each year. Since its beginning in 1993, Jill and a generous troupe of volunteers have worked tirelessly to restore dignity to "career women who specialize in the home," emphasizing that "motherhood isn't a second-rate occupation."[28] In her book, *Professionalizing Motherhood*, Jill says:

> To send children into adulthood who are morally responsible and emotionally mature takes an incredible amount of time and energy. It takes intelligence and skill. To run all the activities of a typical family requires an ability to manage resources of time, money and energy. We must not devalue the responsibilities of caring for a family. We must take this job seriously. *The profession of motherhood is about devoting your good mind and exceptional skills to the nurturing of your family.*[29]

Joy of joys! I didn't have to be a career woman in order to: (1) pursue my parenting in a professional manner, and (2) be engaged in an enterprise outside of mothering my own children, as are Jill and all the Hearts at Home volunteers. Ephesians 2:10 says, "For we are God's workmanship, created in Christ Jesus to do good works, which God prepared in advance for us to do." Not only did God create us as precious, handmade gifts (as in Chapter 2: God's will is that we know and believe this truth), he has prepared a work for us to do—and not just *any* work, a *good* work. Our primary work, for those of us with children, is to be mothers, *professional* mothers. But clearly God created room in a family for mom to make use of her unique gifts and talents, too. A mother's responsibilities to God, spouse, and children are top priority, but not exclusive priority.

Susan Maushart writes in *The Mask of Motherhood* that "Motherhood can be, and almost always is, performed alongside other forms of work. Indeed, the practice of something called 'full-time mothering'—in which a woman's sole responsibilities in communal life revolve exclusively around home and child—is an historical aberration of twentieth-century industrialized life."[30] I looked to the Bible to affirm Maushart's statement and found a great example of a godly mother in Proverbs 31; verse 28 says, "Her children arise and call her blessed; her husband also and he praises her." But mothering was not all this woman did. She was a manufacturer, an importer, a seamstress, a merchant, and a farmer. The Proverbs 31 mother was neither a housewife nor a career woman, yet clearly she used her gifts and talents to build up the Kingdom of God both inside *and* outside her home.

After straightening out my misconceptions of housewives and career women, I felt a lot less guilty about my life. I answered God's calling to write and photo-illustrate children's books and it has not compromised my mothering, but rather has strengthened my organizational skills, sharpened my focus on the profession of motherhood, recharged my passion for photography, and given me a renewed sense of self.

Today, when I am asked what I do, I say that I am a home-based, family-centered mom. By being home-based I mean that I choose to put the needs of my home and the people that live there ahead of the needs of an employer. Being home-based means that home is the base for all my operations. Being home-based is not synonymous with being unenlightened or uninterested in the opportunities of the working world. It does not mean that I couldn't cut it in the work-place or that I love soap operas or getting my nails done, or that I think only of my children. It does not mean that I do nothing out-side of my home or that I cannot bring in income or go outside of my home to engage in business other than that tied directly to my chil-dren. That I am a family-centered mom means that I choose, before any specific opportunity comes up, to be available to meet the needs of my family first and that every other activity flows from and after that central priority. "Home-based and family-centered" moms is the term I will use in place of "at-home" moms for the duration of this book to describe moms who are mothering full time, but who also run home-based businesses; enjoy flexible, part-time employment; vol-unteer; do home-schooling; attend school themselves; or are involved in a myriad of activities outside of mothering, because I believe a new term is needed. If you are a woman for whom full-time mothering has come naturally or a woman who has already found great joy and peace in being a hundred percent at home with your children, you may be offended by the admission that I (or any mother) feel myself a better mother now that I am engaged in an enterprise outside of mothering. What am I suggesting by this confession? Does this mean that I think that all mothers should be involved in activities outside of mothering? No, not at all. Especially when the children are young, I feel it is *essential* that a mother make every possible effort to be at home (or as I prefer to say, home-based and family-centered) in order to give her child "mother care" rather than leave her child in "other care." However, as the children get older and start school, and *if* the mother is interested, her activities can expand beyond her home without compromising the well-being of the children, *if* she is able to keep her priorities straight (placing needs of kids before needs of her other activities).

In the span of eight years and five children, I went from a reluctant to a purposeful mother in the eyes of those who are witnessing my motherhood. I know this change has taken place not only because this is what people said about me, but also because I feel at peace with myself. I am no longer a hypocrite, hiding behind different masks. Instead, I enjoy dressing up in many different hats. God revealed that I am about his business whether I am changing a child's diaper, helping with homework, cleaning the kitchen, taking photographs for a children's book, or speaking at a women's conference. If I am doing what God has called me to do, and keeping my family as top priority, then it is all Kingdom work.

Two Kid-Friendly Models of How to Balance Babies and Business

Kate Taylor is a modern Proverbs 31 woman who chose the career-postponement or seasonal model of balancing family/work.

Taylor is the sister of internationally famous singer/songwriter James Taylor. Most of the world, minus Martha's Vineyard where Taylor lives with her family, has not heard from Kate since 1979 when she released her third and last album with Columbia Records. Why not? Because, according to a feature article in the *Cape Cod Times*, "twenty years ago she made a decision that her recording career would take back seat to raising daughters Aretha, 18, Elizabeth, 24, and Aquinnah, 26." The article quotes Taylor as saying, "The family life became our most creative effort."[31]

Kate Taylor had a blossoming music career complete with family connections and, one would assume, the financial ability to provide great childcare for her children. She could have "had it all." But she *chose* not to. Now, at the age of fifty, Taylor is releasing her first album in twenty-one years titled *Beautiful Road*. Taylor is a great role model for every talented woman who aspires to live life in its season and mother full time when her children are at home. Most of all, Taylor is a good role model for her own three daughters who have learned firsthand that they are worth their mother's love and nurturance.

Leslie is a modern example of a Proverbs 31 mother who has chosen the flexible, home-based work model of balancing family and work. As an advocate for stay-at-home moms, Leslie writes and edits *Hearts at Home*, a monthly publication for the Hearts at Home ministry. Angie Peters, in her book *Celebrate Home*, interviewed Leslie. After discussing with Leslie how she began her at-home career with two children and why she became involved with the Hearts at Home organization after having her children, Peters asks her what I believe is the all-important question: "Does this work [running a newsletter for mothers at home] detract from your mothering career?"[32] In other words, isn't it a bit hypocritical to say you are an "at-home mother" but then to be running a magazine for at-home mothers?

Leslie's answer confirmed, once again, that I was wrong in thinking that being at home meant being a housewife, literally staying in the house while being focused on the kids at all times. She sums up in the interview:

> I have a real strong devotion to my mission, my ministry. I have to remember that after my children are grown, that I will still have to have something that is me. Even apart from my husband. I feel like it is a ministry of the Lord that I am part of that. He [God] has called me to do this. And I have to serve him first. My children are a part of my ministry, but there has to be a balance.[33]

Leslie was not pursuing a career she had worked hard to establish and felt she just couldn't give up. She was not out shopping, or traveling for pleasure, or doing whatever else made her happy—instead of mothering her children. She was obeying God's call to part-time employment in a ministry and her involvement was not hurting, but helping, her motherhood.

Mother-Care and Other-Care

Some mothers (like Kate) become better mothers by focusing completely on their children and their home and letting the work world pass them by for a season. Some mothers (like Leslie) become better at mothering by having an outlet for their individuality that can contract and expand as the seasons of motherhood fluctuate. However, it is rarely, if ever, the case that a woman becomes a better mother by focusing on her career full time and leaving her children in the care of others for most of the day. It is the issue of childcare that makes the strongest case against continuing in full-time employment after a woman becomes a mother, no matter how much she enjoys her work, needs an outlet for her talents, or needs the additional income. Childcare is an issue of critical importance to our society that the feminist movement has not been able to address in a manner that keeps children's welfare as top priority, not mothers' convenience or employers' ease.

Of course, there are mothers who work to support the family. This has been true throughout history. However, I am going to address at length in Chapter 6 the topic of money and the reasons that women work and will concentrate here on affirming mothers who are trying to make childcare decisions that benefit their children. I do this because it seems that there are mothers out there who truly believe that the care of their children is better yielded to paid "experts" rather than undertaken by themselves.

Dr. Brenda Hunter provides an example of this misguided thinking in her book *Home by Choice*:

> Betsy [a new mother planning to put her newborn in daycare when he was three weeks old] believed that her baby needed to be socialized through contacts with older adults and children. What she didn't know was that during his first year her child needed a "close, continuous, intimate" relationship with her far more than the company of others. Child development experts indicate that children do not engage in peer play until they are about two years old.[34]

There are three main reasons a mother becomes comfortable leaving, even desiring to leave (as Betsy did), the care of her children to some ever-shifting patchwork of daycare, schoolcare, nannycare, or neighborcare: (1) she is working to support her family in a job that does not allow for children to be nearby; (2) she is genuinely unaware of her own, irreplaceable importance; or (3) she is aware of her own importance, but is willing to pay the personal price of not acting on her knowledge.

Regarding the first type of reasoning, everything I've written so far in this book reveals that I believe that a woman needing to support a family should do everything in her power to rearrange her work to accommodate the needs of her children, not the other way around. To the extent that a woman can or is willing to rearrange her work schedule to give her children high priority, I believe that her efforts will be blessed. Regarding the third type of reasoning, there is no clever argument or logic that would talk a woman out of what she sees as her "right" to carry on in her career and put her child in daycare, despite knowing the hardship it causes her family. Trying to reconcile this woman's denial and disparate agendas for herself and her family point by point would be like trying to herd cats.

And so, with this book's goal of peacemaking in mind, I will contain my comments on daycare to those that will help mothers whose reasoning falls in category two (simple unawareness). Based on a new awareness of their own value, it is this category of mothers that I hope will embrace motherhood more fully and peacefully. With improved understanding and confidence in their own importance, I believe that these moms will be empowered to make work/childcare decisions that are in the best interest of their children, even if it means standing against the cultural storm.

The authors of *Irreducible Needs of Children*, Dr. T. Berry Brazelton, professor emeritus at Harvard Medical School, and Dr. Stanley Greenspan, clinical professor at George Washington University of Medicine, have done research which they hope will increase societal awareness of the primary importance of the work of motherhood. Their work helps dispel the "socialization" myths brought up in Dr. Brenda Hunter's example of a misinformed mother who thought her child "needed" to be in daycare. "Parents cannot underestimate the importance of their role in these early years," say Drs. Brazelton and Greenspan. "The way a parent nurtures a baby has a profound effect on how the child develops."[35] In their book, the doctors place "ongoing nurturing relationships" as number one among the irreducible needs of a child, stating that "Every baby needs a warm, intimate relationship with a primary caregiver over a period of years, not months or weeks. This is far more important to emotional and intellectual development than early cognitive training or educational games. If this relationship is absent or interrupted, a child can develop disorders of reasoning, motivation and attachment. Infants, toddlers and preschoolers need these nurturing interactions most of their waking hours."[36]

Thomas Hayden is a columnist who draws the same conclusion as Drs. Brazelton and Greenspan. In the Fall/Winter 2000 edition of Newsweek's *Your Baby* magazine, Hayden expands on the effect of environment on a child's development by questioning the myth that our destinies are preordained by our genes (a myth that undermines the work of mothering). Hayden opened his article, "A Sense of Self," by asking, "Is it nature or is it nurture that forms a newborn into the person he or she becomes?" "Let's start with the genes," he writes. "The story of the 90s was that scientists were discovering 'genes' for all sorts of personality traits—happiness, aggressiveness, neuroticism, sexual orientation, risk taking and so on. Virtually all those findings, or their significance have been disputed in the scientific community...." Continuing to review current medical thought on the importance of genetics in determining personality, Hayden quotes geneticist Dean Hamer of the National Institutes of Health as saying, "We come in part ready-made from the factory." But Hayden goes on to say that genes do not act in a vacuum. "The information they carry, according to the rigorous studies now emerging, can be quieted or amplified depending on what environment a child lives in—and for infants, 'environment' means to a large extent the adults they depend on."[37]

The time we spend creating a loving home is not insignificant, even if it is filled with many mundane tasks. Home is the environment—the vital training ground—where our children's personalities can be "quieted or amplified" by our presence and our loving direction. We (mothers and fathers) create that loving home environment by nurturing our children though intimate, ongoing relationships that other-care providers will never be able to duplicate.

The bottom line? Children need mothers, not a string of caregivers. For the children's sake, it is worth the necessary efforts and sacrifices a mother must make to care for her children herself. For one mother, that sacrifice may be learning to live on a single income. For another mother it may be learning to work at odd hours while the children are sleeping. Whatever the sacrifices are for you, remember: your children, my children, our children are worth it.

Perhaps you have struggled, as I did, with the housewife image which is really a hybrid of popular media and feminist expectations of motherhood. Perhaps your struggle, as did mine, led you to deny parts of yourself, to plunge headfirst into being a housewife and to attempt to become who you were not. Perhaps your struggle led you to work at your career even harder after having children, just to prove that you were definitely not a housewife. Whichever the case, I'll bet you have, uncomfortably, worn several different masks in the struggle.

If you are interested in trying the family/work balance model of involvement in flexible activities at the same time that you are in a season of full-time mothering, the first thing to do is to pray for God's direction. Prayer based on Matthew 6:33 is what led me to peace with my struggles: "But seek first his kingdom and his righteousness, and all these things will be given to you as well." By seeking God, through prayer, a simple discernment process of discovering God's call evolved into what I call "Identifying the Three 'Ps' in Your Parenting Pod." You simply ask and honestly answer these questions: (1) What is my Purpose? (2) What am I Passionate about? and (3) What is my Personality type? Earlier in this chapter I briefly mentioned four specific types of activities that provide personal outlets that are compatible with full-time motherhood: (1) volunteering, (2) home-based businesses or flexible employment outside the home, (3) home schooling, and (4) continuing education. I believe these types of activities combine well with motherhood because (1) they are flexible, accommodating to the unpredictable nature of family life, (2) they can be as broad or as narrow as one likes, suited to a mother's purpose, passion, and personality, (3) they can be expanded or contracted to match one's mothering season, and (4) the need for childcare is minimal or nonexistent.

As you go about uncovering the three "Ps" in your parenting pod, whether you are considering taking on responsibilities outside of mothering for self-enrichment or additional income, or shifting your focus from a career to mothering so as to give higher priority to your children, consider how your three "Ps" might fit into these categories of activities. If you are taking on responsibilities outside of mothering for the first time, be careful not to swing to the extreme of full-time involvement in anything lest your children suffer the loss of their mother.

As you begin, do so with the blessed assurance, found in Philippians 1:6, that God has not made a mistake by giving you a child: "Being confident of this, that he who began a good work in you will carry it on to completion until the day of Christ Jesus."

Your Purpose

Stephen Covey is an expert in leadership training. The second habit, described in his book *The Seven Habits of Highly Effective People,* is to "Begin with an End in Mind."[38] That is, establish an inner guidance system at the heart of your purpose in life and for the whole of your life so that you can "examine in the context of this whole (i.e., your purpose) what really matters most to you."[39] Covey encourages his readers to come up with a "mission statement" for themselves and for their families that will provide structure and clarification for every decision that is made in regard to the individuals and to the family. Here's the thing. If you don't have a purpose, a specific mission statement, how are you going to recognize God's custom-fit call when it comes? Look around at the ways other mothers are living. There are a lot of ways to know God, to love God, and to serve God.

What is your purpose in having children? This is a humbling, hard question, but be as intentional and specific in answering it as you can be. In the end, what do you hope to have accomplished? Did you have children for their benefit or yours? If it was for your benefit in the beginning, are you now willing to change your purpose to benefit them? Another humbling question: Why are you searching outside of your mothering duties for a calling, a purpose for your life? To purify your intentions, ask yourself another hard question: Is it for intellectual stimulation? To use your gifts and talents? To provide or to supplement your family's income? To save for a vacation or to purchase a house? To fill a need in your community? They can all be good and valid reasons. Money, for example, is not the most important reason to begin a home-based business if what you really need is a vehicle to express your talents.

"After paying for insurance, I don't make a ton of money with my dance class," Diane allows, "but giving this class gives me a little bit of a break. It forces me to take care of myself, to play and not always feel so responsible as a mom. It helps me to go back to my responsibilities recharged and reenergized." On the other hand, making money may be an important reason for your involvement in a business. If it is, how much money do you need? Make a business plan. Don't work overtime to get more money if it means being away from your children longer and the additional money is not necessary for you to accomplish your purpose.

Your mission statement, your purpose, will become your "inner guidance system," as Covey puts it, in answering all the specific questions that come up in the context of discerning your purpose.

Your Passion

The second "P" to consider is what is your passion? What is it that you cannot stop doing? Is it gardening? Music? Being with older people? Investment banking? At this point don't restrict yourself to things that you think will work out well with mothering. Yes, some activities (professions, skills, interests) are much more compatible with raising children, but mothering is done in seasons. The mothering demands placed on you today will be different from those of tomorrow.

For this passion brainstorming session go wild. Think big. What is it that you love? If you enjoyed what you were doing before you had children, if it is your passion, look for a way to use your knowledge and your skills without neglecting your children. If you did not enjoy what you were doing before children, then please, start something new! In her list of ten life lessons for students graduating from college, Maria Shriver lists *Pinpoint Your Passion* as number one. "Trust your gut," she says, "no matter what you expect your parents or teachers or anyone else will think of your choice."[40]

Your Personality

The third "P" is your Personality. There is a plethora of books and type-indicator tests available for you to take in order to determine your personality. One of the most common is the Myers-Briggs Type Indicator. You may have taken this test in high school, as I did, in trying to determine what you might like to study in college and what career to pursue.

Cynthia Ulrich Tobias has written a book called *The Way They Learn* in which she helps parents identify and appreciate the unique learning styles of their children so that they can identify the natural strengths and tendencies that each child possesses. Not surprisingly the first chapter of her book asks parents to identify their own learning styles before trying to identify those of their children![41]

Helen T. Boursier's book on evangelism, *Tell It With Style*, explores the implications of your personality on your ability to share the Gospel with others with differing personality styles. Boursier emphasizes three excellent points in her book: (1) Determining your personality does not mean putting yourself in a "neatly categorized or figured out" box. "When you look inside and really see your strengths and weaknesses, you will know what needs adjusting,"[42] Boursier says. We always have the choice to change. (2) Our personalities are not completely unique and isolated from those around us; we all exist on a continuum of personality styles. In other words, just because *you* are outgoing and funny does not mean that I am not. Our personalities are relative to the personalities of those around us.[43] (3) You are a "personality milkshake." No matter what system you use to identify your personality type, asserts Boursier, "you will find that you have one main personality style, with a secondary one following close behind." Tim LaHaye (author of *Spirit-Controlled Temperament*) calls these "personality blends."[44]

I highly recommend that you take a personality test or get a book like one of those mentioned that are helpful for taking personal inventory. The self-knowledge one gains is richly rewarding and infinitely helpful in making good choices about relationships and responsibilities. For example, I figured out from Tobias's book that I process information in a highly sequential manner.[45] This explains why I'd rather bring my volunteer work for the church library home where I can do it step-by-step as time allows. My personality lends itself to creating order out of chaos. I don't need someone (or something) to provide order for me. A fellow library volunteer processes information in a random manner. This means that she would rather go to the library to do her work because the environment is already highly structured, allowing her to accomplish her work in no particular sequence. Her personality lends itself to impulsive creativity. Understanding our different personalities makes us a good team. She spontaneously comes up with very creative ideas, and I lay out the plans to see that the ideas become a reality.

It can be quite fun to take a personality test with your spouse or with a group of friends. Their strengths and your own might really surprise you. As far as learning about your weaknesses goes—well, I find that it is definitely easier to read of my weaknesses in some objective report of test results than it is to hear them verbalized during a personal conflict with someone I love!

Focus Questions for Making Peace

1. Insert one of the following mathematical signs ($<$, $>$, or $=$) into the equation below:

Mothering _____ Career/Work

Why do you feel this way?

2. If you have put your child in daycare situations, which of the following best fits your reasoning?

- You are providing necessary income for your family in a job that does not allow your child to be nearby.

- You truly feel it is necessary for your child.

- You know it is not necessary for your child, but you find it easier than altering your work schedule.

3. Does understanding how important you are to your child make you want to reevaluate your current child-care decisions? Why or why not? If yes, how?

4. How has learning about and beginning to understand your three "Ps" helped bring peace to your mothering journey? List at least one helpful point for each "P" and put a star next to the one that was the most helpful.

- *Purpose* (Formulating my purpose has helped me....)

- *Passion* (Discovering my passion has helped me....)

- *Personality* (Understanding my personality has helped me....)

Chapter 4

Successfully Wasting My Education: Motherhood and Higher Education

A s I have come to experience the fluidity of life, the ebb and flow, and the intertwining of the miraculous and the mundane, I can see that education is very important. I have a Bachelor of Science degree in Physical Geography. My education trained me to read and make maps. That means I can tell you what's where and why. That means that the apex of my professional career—begun as a newspaper reporter and photographer in high school and continued by studying geography in college, plus my natural love of the camera—would have been to become a travel photographer for *National Geographic* magazine. But then I had kids.

I had been out of college for eight months and employed in my field for all of three weeks when we found out that we were expecting our first baby. *Three weeks.* I worked during the entire pregnancy, but ultimately I knew that I wasn't interested in the daycare routine. Unfortunately, my choice to care for my child myself meant that there were no great projects or early promotions directed my way, since I shared my intentions honestly with my boss.

If there was one, most difficult hurdle for me in making peace with motherhood, it was choosing not to use my college degree. I felt as if I had wasted four years of higher education and, unfortunately, there were many people in my life who were quite eager to tell me that I had indeed. But had I? Our society has caged motherhood in an erroneous paradigm—a paradigm that says that being a mother encompasses only mindless housework, serving Kool-Aid at snack time, and taxiing the kids around all day—the whole "housewife" issue of Chapter 3. These are activities, our society says, that don't require a college education. But I have discovered that this is not true. Hardly a day goes by that I don't use some information I gained in college as I parent my children. In fact, as motherhood has unfolded and I have found myself entrusted with five precious babies, I certainly wish I had spent a few *more* years at the old alma mater taking classes like child development or child psychology.

With her doctorate degree in music education and music therapy nearly complete, Dr. Mary Ann Froehlich and her husband found out that they were expecting for the first time. On the threshold of completing years of formal education, Froehlich chose to "trade a promising music career for diapers and shopping carts."[46] After finishing her degree and in the midst of raising three children she wrote about conquering the guilt of "wasting her education" in a book titled *What's a Smart Woman Like You Doing in a Place Like This?* Here is what "Dr. Mom" says:

> When I was working and in graduate school, more than one person asked me why I was working so hard. Wasn't it all going to be wasted when I stopped to have a family? They made motherhood sound like a prison term, a bad pill to swallow, a time for putting life on hold. Raising a family was posed as the antithesis of growing, learning, thinking, and contributing a specialization. I have found family life to be quite the opposite. Not only is this the most enjoyable time of my life, but also my children are the most stimulating and challenging teachers I've had yet, and they have tapped every resource in my background.[47]

Certainly it would have been possible for Dr. Froehlich to begin her self-described "journey into becoming a professional at home"[48] without a doctoral degree, but for her it seems to have been the process of acquiring a formal education that actually trained her to take motherhood by storm rather than letting false guilt get in the way and demoralize her.

Dr. Froehlich's story is encouraging. She is one of many new-style mothers who are proving the "wasting-your-education" argument to be completely wrong as it relates to choosing to be more available to our children rather than to a boss. "Education is an *atmosphere*, a *discipline*, a *life*," Susan Schaeffer Macaulay says, paraphrasing educational reformer Charlotte Mason in her book *For the Children's Sake*.[49] There are three ways in which education, specifically an advanced education, is the best preparation for, not wasted on, motherhood: (1) in developing a woman's self-confidence, (2) in increasing her family/work choices, and (3) in helping her to educate her own children.

Self-Confidence

I now know, twelve years after graduation, that the specific facts I learned in college are trifles compared with the confidence I gained by completing my degree. Completing a college education has given me the confidence to begin my own home-based business, the confidence to stand up and speak my beliefs whether in a letter-to-the-editor or to a crowd of women at a mothers' conference, the confidence to begin educating my children at home. Karen expressed similar thoughts after finishing her Ph.D. in biochemistry one year and then becoming a full-time mother the next. "I am more confident in myself and in my intelligence since my struggle with my Ph.D. It was the hardest, most grueling, painful experience I have ever accomplished, but the key is that I accomplished it. I know I am capable of meeting a very difficult challenge." Karen told me this just a few months *after* enduring a high-risk pregnancy and a risky labor and childbirth!

"Having a college education has been crucial in helping me be a mother," says Carrie, another well-educated mom. "My degree was a masters in mathematics and computer science which sounds like it would have no relevance to motherhood, but the self-confidence it has given me has been invaluable."

College equipped me to explore a problem and to propose a solution. College has given me the confidence and skills to do research in order to fill the gaps in my understanding of parenting, being a spouse, writing, or taking photographs. College allowed me to *choose* mothering as a full-time profession, because I legitimately had (and still do have) other options. Although it is not a completely nice thing to reveal about myself, knowing I have not settled for but have rather chosen to be a mother is a huge boost to my confidence when things get tough and I question the wisdom of mothering full time.

I am nowhere near my goal of shooting assignments for *National Geographic*, nor will I be any time soon, but this is because I have *chosen* to put the real needs of my children above the supposed need to use my education to its fullest. In simple terms, time spent in college gave me an opportunity to develop myself independently from my family of origin, my future husband and children, and my future bosses. This development time bolstered my self-confidence. Ideally, for all women still unencumbered by the pressures of a career or a family, college can be a richly rewarding time of experiencing new people, ideas, and cultures, and of gaining confidence in handling these experiences.

Increased Family/Work Choices

Thanks in part to the vast accomplishments of the feminist movement in the United States, employment opportunities for women have multiplied far beyond the traditional occupations of nurse or teacher. Today a woman takes for granted the idea that she can be employed in just about any job she would like—as long as she is qualified for it. Qualification is the door to opportunity for which a college degree is often the key. Without a qualifying degree, that is, a specific amount of classroom preparation for a specialty symbolized by the conferring of a formal degree, many great, flexible, work-around-family jobs are simply out of a mother's reach. Having an advanced degree not only opens the door to many job opportunities, it also prepares a woman to make good choices concerning the use of those opportunities.

Carrie, the mom with a master's degree in mathematics/computer science, explained, "I finished college and had a full career as a computer software engineer before I had my first baby. I also taught at a community college for five years before becoming a stay-at-home mom full time for the past seven years. I know that even though I am not current in my field, someday, if I want, I can go back and have another full career. I know that I can do anything I set my mind to and that confidence has given me the freedom to choose motherhood as my current career."

The value of education in providing choices and as preparation for making good choices about one's life (including motherhood), not just about a particular career, is seen most clearly in the Developing World. In a list of "Ten Urgent Issues for the Children of the New Millennium," compiled by the Christian relief organization World Vision, primary education was ranked third in order of importance after a livable income and food for all.[50] In listing the benefits of education in the Developing World, World Vision comments:

> Education is the single most critical element in combating poverty, empowering women, protecting children from exploitation, and promoting human rights and democracy. Educated girls marry later and are better prepared physically and mentally for motherhood. A mother who understands the importance of health, nutrition, and sanitation can protect her family from preventable illnesses. Parents with even

basic education have better employment opportunities, enabling them to provide for their families and educate their own children. Children equipped with basic literacy and numeracy, as well as more advanced, complex skills for living, have a firm foundation for learning through-out life.[51]

World Vision has plainly experienced the benefits of primary education in a woman's/mother's ability to make good choices about life's basics—food, shelter, and clothing. How much more plainly can we see that having some advanced education can better prepare women for the (perhaps) even more complex choices of mothering in the Developed World.

I forget, now, who it was that led me to believe that I would be wasting my education if I didn't pursue full-time employment in the area of my degree immediately after graduating, and without any breaks thereafter. The more important question is, why did I believe them for so long? Christian financial advisor Larry Burkett states quite strongly in his book *Women Leaving the Workplace:*

> The whole idea that being a stay-at-home mom is a waste of an educa-tion is an absurd notion. If what a woman learns in school is not appli-cable to raising the next generation, then the school is at fault—not the mom. To allow this deception to continue, that somehow raising children is a waste of an education, is not only wrong, it can be very harmful, because it places false guilt on many women.[52]

That is not to say that reverse guilt should be placed on moms who do not have an advanced education; it should not. Education should be placed within the context of all of one's circumstances and ambitions, and be looked at as a life-long process. All things being equal, however, having specific skills, marketable abilities, and/or advanced education does help; it does increase our choices.

Educating Our Children

I want to consider, now, how having a college degree can help us best educate our own children. The truth is that parents, as extraordinary or ordinary as they may be, are the primary and practical educators of their children no matter where the kids learn to read and write. Every teacher with whom my husband and I have ever had a conference has, without blinking, given us both the initial blame and the initial credit for what our children did and did not know.

Education starts at home. It starts with teaching love, trust, compassion, and all the virtues that will serve a person as he or she grows into a valuable member of society. As Christian moms our most important educational duty is to teach our children, in word and in deed, about the saving love of Jesus. It is also, as Gladys Hunt, author of *Honey for a Child's Heart*, puts it, to influence them to have an "uncommon delight in what is good and true and beautiful—and an uncommon commitment to it."[53]

On top of establishing these foundational aspects of education, parents help with homework, book reports, and science fair projects. Parents run the shuttle bus between school and after-school activities. Parents gather in PTA groups and para-school committees to voice their opinions about curriculum, sports, testing, and new building projects. On all levels, parent participation is of vital importance to a child's success in school. Is an advanced education *required* for a mom to do a great job at helping her kids to learn themselves? No. Absolutely not. But, in short, World Vision's summary of the value of education for a mother in the Developing World applies to the Developed World, too: All else being equal, an educated mother is better able to help educate her own children.

Home-Schooling

A direct application of this knowledge is seen in the phenomenal growth of the Home-schooling Movement. Not since before one-room schoolhouses dotted our great land in the beginning of the 1800s have so many parents, particularly mothers, taken upon themselves the direct tutelage of their children.

Home-schooling is taking our nation by storm and by surprise. Who would have predicted, even ten years ago, that a whopping 1.5 to 1.9 million children[54] would be educated at home between 2000–2001, with the numbers rising twenty-five percent a year?[55] Certainly not I, as I gazed at my first newborn, Nicole, and considered our future together. I thought I would prepare her for school up to age five. Then, I thought, she would hop on the school bus, just as I had, and her education would be taken care of, as simple as that.

But a change is afoot in our society. Many children (more than 1.7 million) will never ride a school bus or sit in a classroom in order to become educated. They will have siblings as classmates, parents as teachers, sports teams and church as their primary sources of extra-familial socialization, and libraries and the Internet as their most consistent connection to the world beyond their home.

I address the topic of home-schooling here not because it is trendy or sensational to do so, but because our family recently became a part of that growing population. My husband and I have always believed in the concept or the theory of home-schooling, sort of like we believed in the "concept" of changing the oil in our car every 3,000 miles. "Sounds good. It would probably even help the car. But to actually do it? Gee whiz. Golly. Hmm. That, well that…that would require a sincere effort. I mean, if it's not broke, why fix it?" To be honest, it was a shaky step from theory to practice in deciding to home-school. The majority of our experiences with private and public school systems were very positive. But, now that we have been home-schooling the three school-aged children for almost three years, I can see how much better home education has been for the whole family. It is a lot of work, mind you, but having had three kids in six different school systems since our oldest started school, I can tell you that staying in tune with their teachers, classmates, curriculum, and after-school activities was already a lot of work!

Home-schooling is no small undertaking. It takes a teachable heart and a willingness to take extraordinary educational initiative on behalf of your child. It means learning to patiently and kindly answer the "What about socialization?" question from family, friends, and complete strangers for the millionth time. It takes a peerless combination of love and conviction. Home-schooling is, as Dana Mack reports in her book *Assault On Parenthood*,

> ...a dramatic statement of a new kind of commitment to family life, and of a conviction that a rich family life is our greatest reward. Home-schooling is one aspect of a new vision of family life that equates family time with children's well-being, and that puts family intimacy and parent-child bonds before self-realization and economic gain.[56]

I want to emphasize that it is not necessary to have a teaching degree or a college education to home-school. Many home educators do not have these credentials and still do an exceptional job of educating their children. But, having a college degree myself or, more specifically, having both the self-confidence and the knowledge I gained while earning my degree, gave me the *beforehand* certitude I needed to say, "Yes, I can home-school."

In her last statement (about family intimacy and parent-child bond before self-realization and economic gain), Mack converges in her book on the sum total of my search for peace in mothering as it relates to both using my college education and diligently training up my children. I, *my* ego, *my* self-actualization, *my* gain, and *my* use of *my* education are far less important than my faithfully meeting the needs of the family that I desired, I cocreated, and that I now have. Mack's statement is where the rubber hit the road for me in comprehending the audacity of the idea of the "wasting" of my education on the parenting of my children. What good is my education if I don't use it to profit my children's lives—to enrich them with the knowledge and love of God and the awesome world around them? A million dollars gained by my having the best job my education could provide wouldn't teach them that love, but I can. So, I guess, if mothering is a waste of an advanced education, then I am happily and successfully wasting mine.

Once again, all things being equal, having a college education does help—it does increase our confidence in and our choices for either overseeing our children's education or educating them ourselves.

Of all the ways one can use an education, I believe with Larry Burkett that shaping the next generation, bettering the world for one's own children and grandchildren, is one of the most noble and beneficial uses to society as a whole. We can literally change the world one choice, one child, at a time.

By making *one* choice to cast off the false guilt of wasting our educations we are free to start investing our schooling, our lives, our love, our aggregate knowledge on our children until we have successfully wasted our education. Soon we will find ourselves like Dr. Mary Ann Froehlich, Dr. Karen, and Carrie experiencing that the best use of any and all of our education is in raising our children. Or like Mother Teresa of Calcutta with a world of just "one, one, and one"[57] children who are changed because of our *one* life not stifled by the false guilt of wasting our educations.

Focus Questions for Making Peace

1. Read Deuteronomy 6:7, Proverbs 22:6, and Titus 2:3–5 and record from each verse at least one spiritual insight into the lifelong value of education.

2. Write down at least one way that you are (or could be) using your education, not wasting it as a mother.

3. List the people (or organizations) who have made you feel as though motherhood is a waste of your college degree. Why do you suppose they felt this way? Is it valid to apply their feelings to your current life? Why or why not?

Part II

Sharing Our Family-Centered Focus

Chapter 5

Spiritual Peace:
Spiritual Constraints of Motherhood

During the years we lived in Berkeley, California, "the perfect morning" would begin with a visit to our favorite café, Café Roma. After indulging the kids in freshly baked muffins and hot chocolates mounded with whipped cream and treating myself to a mocha latté, we would cross the street to Monterey Market, a modified open-air fruit market, and relish fresh produce brought in that morning from Salinas Valley. With a stroller full of a colorful harvest from the fruit market, we would amble up the narrow, Eucalyptus-lined street to a Greek bakery and pick up a baguette of the world's greatest sweet bread. The morning was made complete by winding our way farther up the road to a community playground where we snacked on our goodies and played until it was time for afternoon naps. I enjoyed these mornings so much because I was able to combine practical errands and fun activities in a way that satisfied both the kids and myself.

One sunny morning while my four children and I were beginning our perfect morning of errands among the purple flowers on the outdoor patio of Café Roma, two very tired-looking women in their mid-to-late thirties came into the café and sank into chairs opposite our table. One of the pair had skillfully maneuvered a large, old-fashioned baby buggy onto the patio and squeezed it next to a table. There must have been a sleeping infant somewhere in the buggy, although I could not see around the extravagant accessories and packages in order to be sure. These world-weary women began a conversation that went something like this:

> "My life is just one thing (the kids). It is coming and going and doing whatever comes up," sighed the pilot of the mammoth buggy.
> "I know what you mean," the second lady sighed in harmony with the first. "I'd like to work for a non-profit. A women's organization. You know, the kind where I could wear long skirts and cotton tops."
> "Yes!" echoed the buggy pilot. "My husband gets mad when I say, 'But *you* can go out to lunch.' 'You can, too,' he tells me, but he is wrong. I mean go to lunch *by myself*! I always have the kids with me."

I stopped listening and started praying for these two mothers. I had been where they were now, imprisoned in a pity-party. I cried for them. The contrast between how marvelous I felt about doing morning errands with my four little sticky-faced muffin-eaters and the oppressive burden these moms felt about their morning punctuated the need for me to pray for them. There was an obvious lack of joy in motherhood for these women that went deeper than just sharing with a friend about *one* bad day. They were spiraling into a despairing conversation that they had probably had a thousand times before with every other mother they had ever met. Chances were that this conversation wouldn't yield any more positive solutions than any of their previous conversations. Both would go home more rather than less discouraged by their time spent together sipping cappuccino.

Why do we do this to ourselves? Why is the default discussion of any women's gathering about how hard we have it and how much easier everyone else has it? Why does every mothers' get-together degenerate into a gripe session? To be sure there is some truth involved. I have marveled at single mothers overcoming incredible obstacles to give their children the best possible home life. I have observed mothers with seven and eight children patiently home-schooling the entire bunch. I have, myself, experienced the trials of having between one and five children at home with me twenty-four hours a day, seven days a week for more than eleven years. Trust me, I know the claustrophobic condition so much togetherness with children can create in a mother's life! Motherhood is not easy. But, having worked outside the home and having frequently visited my husband at his place of work, I know that the office or job site is no utopia either.

Faithfulness Brings More Peace Than Successfulness

What we need to make spiritual, emotional, and psychological peace with motherhood is not to compare our "To Do" lists with those of our husbands or of other moms, but to adjust our inner selves—our spiritual perspectives. The first thing that needs adjusting is our understanding of success. The glorification of success has caused more than one good mother to lose her balance on the high wire of mothering. Success is god to the world in which we live. Unfortunately, success has many delicate shades of meaning. Success to one is failure to another so that when we set out to be "successful," we quite often end up chasing our tails. Success is really a false god—a stumbling block for us as Christian mothers. After receiving the Nobel Peace Prize, Mother Teresa of Calcutta said, "We are called upon not to be successful but to be faithful."[58] Mother Teresa's words remind us that when we receive a calling from God, say motherhood, we must approach it from a spiritual perspective, *not* a success perspective.

In moving toward our goal of achieving and maintaining peace in God's call to motherhood, we must resist the temptation to evaluate ourselves by the measure of success that the world dangles before us (primarily fame and fortune). Success will never truly satisfy, but obedience to God's biblical will and God's special call to motherhood will enable, empower, energize, *and* satisfy us.

Jesus is Our Center of Gravity

Take a look at Figure 1. It is a photograph of my daughter, Nicole, balancing on a log that has fallen over the water. This photograph is a word picture of the spiritual balancing act in which we are engaged as home-based, family-centered moms. Nicole's center of gravity, somewhere in the middle of her body, is the most important element of her ability to remain balanced on the log. Point number one: Jesus must be my "center of gravity," the most important element of my life, if I am to enjoy peaceful, balanced mothering. He is the ballast around which I must continuously poise and counterpoise my spiritual virtues or "shift my spiritual weight" in order to press forward toward fulfillment of God's call.

The spiritual virtues we must balance—initiative, contentment, and faithfulness—make up the triangle formed by Nicole's arms and a point in space toward which she is walking. Look at Nicole's arms. Near the end of one arm the word *Initiative* is written. Near the end of the other is the word *Contentment*. With the raising or lowering of either arm in opposition to the other, Nicole is able to maintain her center of gravity and therefore her balance. In the same way, alternately taking initiative and being content will often operate in opposition in order to maintain a balanced, peaceful perspective in motherhood.

Initiative

Taking initiative is signing up for a play-group when you move into a new town. Initiative is beginning to volunteer where you see a need. Initiative is resigning from a job that demands fifty to sixty hours per week after your first baby is born. Taking action on a commitment

CONTENTMENT
PSALM 37:7

FAITHFULNESS
PHILIPPIANS 1:6

INTIATIVE
PROVERBS 31:27

SPIRITUAL
CONSTRAINTS

Photograph by Heidi Bratton.

Figure 1, Spiritual constraints

or a decision, despite fear of failure or rejection, is initiative. Initiative is tied to obedience when it is doing what God calls you to do. Initiative is spelled out in Proverbs 31:27: "She watches over the affairs of her household and does not eat the bread of idleness."

Contentment

Being content is also doing what God is calling you to do. It is being satisfied with an e-mail conversation with a good friend when you don't have time for a play-group. It is saying no to a volunteer position you'd love to take on when you are committed to breast-feeding your new baby. It is agreeing to a flexible work schedule as an interim measure while the family is still financially dependent on your income. Contentment is summed up in Psalm 37:7: "Be still before the LORD and wait patiently for him. Do not fret when others succeed in their ways."

Contentment as a plan of action needs a little more explaining than does initiative. Meditate for a minute on the prayerful posture God is giving us in Psalm 37. It is not an anxious, "Oh, what should I do next? Maybe I should do this…or that…or…." Psalm 37 says not to fret or to compare with others. To be content is not a lack of action that is filled in with anxious worry. To be content is a powerful, peaceful type of action, a choice to be grateful in the present that gives us time to prepare for the swing toward initiative when it comes.

Faithfulness

The third point on Figure 1 is out in front of Nicole. It is *Faithfulness*. Nicole's goal is not to stand still on the log, but to move forward. It is the same with motherhood. Our goal is to move forward. To help our children and ourselves grow in healthy, balanced directions. Philippians 1:6 says, "I am confident of this, that he who began a good work in you will carry it on to completion until the day of Christ Jesus."

God has a plan and you are a part of it. Whether you are being called to initiate new activities, to drop some old ones, to be content with the current activities as a part of that plan, be confident, the scripture tells us, because God will complete the plan. With Jesus as your center of gravity, faithfulness as your guide, and initiative and contentment in your activities held in balance, you will move forward with peace.

Finding a Flock of Spiritual Friends

Spiritually, motherhood can be an isolating experience, but it doesn't have to be a solo flight. Like geese that migrate south for the winter in large flocks, fellowship with other Christian mothers can give us strength for the journey, help us to avoid the inevitable spiritual downdrafts, and help us to maintain peace in midair. One of the practical, earthly advantages of being a Christian mother is membership in the church—a local church, and the universal church or the Body of Christ. In addition to weekly church attendance, becoming involved in a Bible study or fellowship group is a great way to grow in and to maintain your spiritual peace. Karen is a Catholic believer married to an Episcopal believer. Once a week she and her husband attend a home Bible study that is hosted by a couple from Karen's church. Karen shares: "This weekly Bible study has helped us by reminding us of God's love as well as facilitating a sharing of experiences between couples. This sharing has provided examples for us in how to face the challenges of today and things that could erode our marriage. It also facilitates communication in our marriage."

Karen's situation is a good example of the universal Body of Christ functioning at its best. Her church didn't offer a mother-specific or even woman-specific Bible study, but it did offer a couples' study.

Even though her husband comes from a different denominational background, they were welcomed by the group from her church and found spiritual companionship in their faith journey. Rarely are there sufficient body count, organizational space, and dynamic energy to have a vibrant women's (much less a mothers-only) ministry in every church in every town. Like Karen, you may need to consider a different type of fellowship within your church, inquire at another Christian church, or look into a parachurch organization in order to find a group that meets your fellowship needs. It depends largely on where you live and which local church you attend.

Each time we have moved to a new state, I have joined a Bible study group—sometimes through our local church, sometimes through parachurch organizations. Like Karen, I have become a richer, more Christ-centered woman because of my involvement in these groups. I have had some great interdenominational experiences and have been blessed by the different perspectives of many believers. I remember a charismatic believer from an Assemblies of God church who continually reminded our group that the Holy Spirit is alive and well, working in our lives this very day. Her confidence in the Spirit's presence picked up mine on days when my feelings told me differently. A Baptist believer reminded us that God is not only our Savior and Friend, but that he is Holy and Just, worthy of all honor and praise. A Catholic believer taught our group how to celebrate Advent and Lent. Her family-centered, non-materialistic ideas spiritually enriched our preparations for Christmas and Easter in immeasurable ways. Frankly, I would be spiritually exhausted, grounded, and shivering somewhere north of the snowline without the spiritual strength that each of these mothers has added to my earthly migration toward heaven.

Unfortunately, some of my experiences in the universal Body of Christ have been distressing, too. One year, having just moved to a new region of the country, I joined a parachurch Bible study because

I was unable to attend the one offered at my church. As the year wore on, it became clear to me that most members of this Bible study attended the host church and it was expected that I would, too, if I were truly being saved through my time spent there. This particular group did not seem as concerned with evangelizing its members as with proselytizing them (converting them to a specific church). The mixing of these two agendas made me very uncomfortable. Fortunately, the teaching leader and I were able to have a few heart-to-hearts and I remained in the group, exchanging wonderful scriptural knowledge and fellowship for the entire time we lived in that town.

I bring up this uncomfortable situation because some of you, in reading my suggestion to fellowship at another church or with a parachurch group if your church does not have a Bible study group, may have inwardly groaned, "Yeah, right. I've tried that before. All those people from different churches just confused me." Well, you're right. Interdenominational relationships are not easy. But it seems that Jesus, knowing that Christian unity would be difficult, still desired us to have it. He prayed specifically for it and us in the Gospel of John:

> These things Jesus spoke; lifting his eyes up to heaven, he said...I pray also for those who will believe in me through their message, that all of them may be one, Father, just as you are in me and I am in you. May they also be in us so that the world may believe that you have sent me...May they be brought to complete unity to let the world know that you sent me and have loved them even as you have loved me. (John 17:20–21, 23)

Divisions that Hurt

Although the Protestant–Catholic division is probably the most glaring wound in the contemporary Body of Christ, divisions within Christianity began, not in Germany on October 31, 1517, with

Martin Luther's protest against the Roman Catholic Church of the Middle Ages, but in the time of the apostles. Listen to what the Apostle Paul has to say to the churches in Corinth concerning divisions among believers:

> For since there is jealousy and quarreling among you are you not worldly? Are you not acting like mere men? For when one says, "I follow Paul," and another, "I follow Apollos," are you not mere men? What, after all, is Apollos? And what is Paul? Only servants through whom you came to believe—as the Lord has assigned to each his task. I planted the seed, Apollos watered it, but God made it grow. So neither he who plants nor he who waters is anything, but only God, who makes things grow. For we are God's fellow workers; you are God's field, God's building. (1 Cor 3:3–7, 9)

Could we not substitute Catholic or Protestant for "follower of Paul or Apollos"? Quaker or Pentecostal? Baptist or Anglican? The denominations *through* which we came to believe? They don't have to be opposite, just different in the way they proclaim Christ, to be guilty of the unholy separation of the Body of Christ that Paul was talking about in his letter to the Corinthians. Tragically, by pledging loyalty to one denomination or to a particular teacher or teaching or to a specific interpretation of the Bible rather than pledging loyalty to Jesus, Christians have allowed denominational factions to splinter the universal church. It is with muddled loyalties, misconceptions, and historical misunderstandings that we approach these factions and enter into ecumenism or the promotion of Christian unity. It may even seem more peaceable to let well enough alone and just beat the path to and from the safety of our own denomination. And yet, Jesus' prayer urges us on.

Toward Healing the Body of Christ

Chuck Colson is a contemporary American Christian who comes from a Baptist tradition. In his best-selling book, *The Body*, Colson says:

> Respecting and appreciating different [Christian] traditions not only teaches us more about our faith, but encourages a measure of theological humility. This attitude helps us avoid the kind of rigid conformity that says everyone must look, act, talk, and think just alike. And this also helps us make the gospel accessible to all people.[59]

Colson is saying what Jesus said in the Gospel of John. Colson calls it "unity with diversity." He agrees that our unity as the universal Body of Christ is a powerful witness to the reality of God's love for each individual. And yet Colson is not hasty to disregard the doctrinal differences.

> Thus, within the orthodox tenets, room remains for our honest, doctrinal disagreement in the church universal. Not for a moment do we expect that Christian bodies will resolve issues like the sacraments, baptism, and ecclesiology on which there has been disagreement for nearly two thousand years.[60]

Since Mr. Colson wrote *The Body*, in 1992, more restoration of the Body of Christ, specifically between Evangelicals and Catholics, has taken place. Colson and Richard John Neuhaus, a convert to Catholicism and the editor of *First Things* magazine, have organized a "loose-knit group of scholars" that produced a document called "Evangelicals and Catholics Together" (ECT).[61] Their pioneering relationship has accomplished much toward the goal of Christian unity about which Jesus spoke by hammering out and issuing two unofficial statements (1994, 1997) on Christian unity that have been endorsed by both Catholic and Evangelical scholars in America.[62] Likewise, addressing the same historic division on October 31, 1999, representatives of the Lutheran World Federation and the Roman Catholic Church signed a historic document called "The Joint Declaration on the Doctrine of Justification." The joint agreement declares that justification is by faith, which compels us to good works. In essence this means "that Catholics and Lutherans agree that justification and salvation are totally free gifts of God and cannot be earned by performing good works, but rather are reflected in good works."[63]

These dialogs and the resulting documents are nothing short of revolutionary. They reflect real healing within the Body of Christ. The progress of that healing is as important to non-believers as it is to believers. The truth is, as Colson writes in *The Body*, "the world isn't looking at our tracts and rallies and telecasts and study manuals. It is looking at us and how we behave. When it fails to see the unity of Jesus' followers—the church—it fails to see the validation that Christ is indeed the Son of the living God."[64]

Our Part in the Healing Process

We do not have to wait for learned theologians and scholars to sign declarations, to bind up all the wounds, large and small, and to give us the big theological thumbs-up sign in order to get together with other believers. As Colson says, "There is no particular reason to expect that they will...until the day when the Lord makes it all clear."[65] We can promote the healing process one friendship at a time in some of the fantastic inter-denominational groups that exist, such as *Mothers of Preschoolers, International* (MOPS), *Community Bible Study* (CBS), and *Hearts at Home,* just to mention a few.

Personally, I'm glad we haven't always found spiritual "one-stop-shopping" at our local church. Having Christian friends of other denominations in the larger Body of Christ has forced me to dive into church teachings and creeds. I have come away with a fairly comprehensive appreciation of the issues of doctrine that really separate us and those issues that are simply nonessential, denominationally-specific behaviors. In doing so, I've seen that we have a lot more in common than not. I've grown stronger in my Christian tradition and more understanding of traditions that are not my own. Again, I am not trying to wash away important *doctrinal* differences that each denomination holds close, but to put *liturgical/behavioral* differences in perspective so as to see if we can't minimize their tendency to tear apart the Body. Once again, like Colson, I don't believe these doctrinal differences will be completely erased in our lifetime. But I do believe, very strongly, that through "experiential education," that is, by living, working, praying, crying together, we will be able to overcome the behavioral differences and achieve a peaceful, *lived* Christian unity among mothers.

Diane Bock is a woman who seeks to apply experiential education to the breaking down of racial prejudice in Los Angeles through a program she founded called "Community Cousins." Bock is quoted in O magazine as saying: "The best way to break down stereotypes is to promote personal contact among people of different groups. If you're going to change the way people think and feel about one another, you have to start by bringing them together."[66] Denominational prejudice is no different than racial prejudice; intolerant legalism is no less codified than Southern segregation laws of the 1960s.[67] According to the Apostle Paul in 1 Corinthians, both prejudice and legalism amount to being "worldly" and "acting like mere men," who do not heal, but do injury to the case of unity. It is time for us to get together, mother-to-mother, shoulder-to-shoulder, and heal the Body.

Thoughts from Theologians Who Are a Part of the Healing Process

In conclusion, let me tie together a string of quotes from several authors whose thoughts on unity within the Body of Christ are filled with a godly grace. Speaking specifically to the Evangelical/Catholic wound, Thomas P. Rausch, S.J., a professor of Catholic theology at Loyola Marymount University, seeks common ground in his book *Catholics and Evangelicals: Do They Share a Common Future?*

> Catholics and Evangelicals share far more than a mutual interest in right to life and family values. Both remain strongly committed to the church's evangelical mission. Both are committed to the central doctrines of the Trinity, the Incarnation, the atoning death and bodily Resurrection of Jesus. And both are concerned with a personally appropriated faith, Catholics through their emphasis on spirituality, Evangelicals through their stress on a personal relationship with Jesus.[68]

Cecil M. Robeck, an Assemblies of God theologian from Fuller Seminary, shares his thoughts on how to soothe the same historically inflamed relationship:

> If I could emphasize just one point, it would be the need for Evangelicals and Roman Catholics to get to know one another. It is in the day-to-day life, in the table talk, in dialogue, in personal sharing where stereotypes will be dealt with, fears will begin to dissipate, and real differences can be settled. If we are not there, yet, perhaps we can at least pause to pray together. There is something that is particularly humbling about kneeling at the foot of the cross before our common Lord and Savior, Jesus Christ. In that act, at the foot of the cross, love is manifested.[69]

Perceiving the entire Body of Christ as crippled by non-essential divisions, Evangelical author Philip Yancey paints a theory-humbling word picture in his book *What's So Amazing About Grace?*

I once read that proportionally the surface of the earth is smoother than a billiard ball. The heights of Mount Everest and the roughs of the Pacific Ocean are very impressive to those of us who live on this planet. But from the view of Andromeda, or even Mars, those differences matter not at all. That is how I now see the petty behavioral differences between one Christian group and another. Compared to a holy and perfect God, the loftiest Everest of rules amounts to a molehill.[70]

In final summary, then, Adam Lum, author of *Luke: New Hope, New Joy*, encapsulates in a sentence the need for each of us to honor the legitimacy of other Christian traditions/behaviors: "There is indeed only one way to God—through Jesus Christ, but there are many ways to Jesus Christ."[71] How very simply, accurately, and peaceably put.

Will you begin to humbly pray for unity within the Body of Christ? Will you who do not have active women's ministries in your church be bold enough to knock on the door of the church or parachurch organization in your area that does? Will you who have active women's ministries reach out to mothers in other Christian denominations, not with the intention of proselytizing or "sheep stealing," but of evangelizing by extending fellowship that is not contingent upon joining your church, and thereby helping to bring about the unity for which Jesus prayed? If you will, I believe we can spiritually strengthen ourselves in the cause of motherhood and be better witnesses of the Gospel to the world.

Focus Questions for Making Peace

1. How would you define success? By your own definition, are you successful?

2. Read Proverbs 16:2–4. What is the Bible's definition of success? Are you successful by this definition?

3. How would you define faithfulness? Read Hebrews 11:1. What is the Bible's definition? Are you faithful by this definition?

4. Read Proverbs 31:27, Psalm 37:7, and Philippians 1:6. Describe the biblical understanding of contentment, initiative, and faithfulness as delineated in these verses.

5. Which of these three virtues is difficult for you? Why?

6. Read Romans 12. Have you experienced a spirit of unity or disunity in your church?

7. If you are involved in Christian fellowship outside of your church, what has helped you to have a spirit of unity with Christians of other denominations? What has hindered your unity in fellowship?

Chapter 6

Maintaining Physical Peace:
Physical Constraints of Motherhood

I f there is one thing I understand it is exhaustion—complete, mind-altering, emotional, spiritual, and physical fatigue. Being bone tired. Our first child, Nicole, was born at 6:02 A.M. after a very tiring, inefficient labor. She was also born with jaundice. An intense through-the-night labor, and my daughter's yellowed condition, began what has ended up being an eleven-year-long siphoning off of all my sleep reserves. Because Nicole needed round-the-clock light therapy for her jaundice, special lamps were fitted to her crib at home. Even at night she had to sleep under the lamps with a tiny little black mask pulled over her eyes. She looked like a miniature Zorro. Due to the bright lights in her crib, she and I didn't softly rock in the moonlight in the wee hours of the morn while she nursed and fell back to sleep. No, we were AWAKE! Playing, eating, and crying (both of us).

She only needed light therapy for about a week, but by that time her wake/sleep pattern had developed to include several extended periods of being awake at night during which she would wail without ceasing if I tried to put her down. Being a first-time mother, I thought this sleep pattern (or lack-of-sleep pattern) must be normal and even after her jaundice lamp was removed, I continued to turn on all the lights in the nursery at night and play with her (as best I could) when she woke up. During the dark and cold months of that first winter of motherhood (Nicole was born at the end of November), I remember going to my sister's home, about an hour's drive away, handing her the baby, and going straight to her room to sleep. I called it "blackout" sleep because I was truly so exhausted I felt as if I had blacked out.

Susan Alexander Yates talks about the problem of fatigue as it is related to the "plummeting self-image" of young mothers in her book *And Then I had Kids*. I could particularly identify with one quote in her book from a mother of three young children who said, "I can't wait until I have some free time and I don't want to use it to take a nap!"[72] I have been there, as have most mothers with young children. There were days, honestly strings of days that added up to months, when my brain was in such a fog, I could not keep my mothering head above water.

"I thought having a child would be like watching my little niece," confesses Maria, mother of four. "Then, when I had my first baby, I couldn't even figure out how to take a shower! Everything became a colossal effort. It was exhausting. I was truly surprised by the physical demands."

"The moment I came home from the hospital with my first child I realized my life was never going to be the same," remembers Carrie, also a mother of four. "All of my preconceived notions of quietly rocking a baby to sleep went out the window. I will never forget a comment my friend Laura made to me. We had both had our first babies within weeks of each other. She said, very seriously, 'Why would anyone have more than one baby?' We were both totally overwhelmed."

Becoming Real

My first pregnancy was a pleasant kind of floating along. My husband and I were awash with idyllic dreams of an adorably perfect baby with absolutely perfect parents paddling our little canoe down a wide, slow-moving river of love. Childbirth was a nosedive over Niagara Falls. Somewhere on my way down to a belly flop, everything that I had previously held together—from temper to mood, to memory, to ability to concentrate and make good decisions, to self-esteem, to a good relationship with my husband—flew out of the boat and randomly cascaded around me. The idyllic days were over as I drifted downstream, sinking more often than floating, trying to reclaim the scattered debris of my life.

Susan Maushart comforts women for whom motherhood has been a nosedive in her book, *The Mask of Motherhood*, with the thought that "a period of healthy disorder is a necessary stage of development on the way to a new and more workable set of assumptions about what we're doing and why we are doing it."[73] The problem, according to Maushart, comes in when we are reluctant to confront the chaos and therefore remain at its mercy rather than use it as an occasion to reorder our lives.

"One child after another quickly challenged everything that I ever believed about myself," says Kathleen, mother of seven. "Each one had their own unique way of exposing my hidden frailties. Though this was not a pleasant experience, it was necessary and a tremendous gift to me. Motherhood often left me feeling weak and overwhelmed, but it also relentlessly drove me to my knees and ultimately to God. In short, my children demand authentic love from me. They are expert at sifting the false, and demanding from me the good that often lies buried. Like the Velveteen Rabbit, they are making me more and more 'real' and for that I am truly thankful."

Rob Parsons, author of an article (and book) entitled "Almost Everything I Need to Know About God I Learned in Sunday School," helped me to gain understanding when he explained why it is that even believers can experience real fear, doubt, and darkness. He says, "God has a way of using our brokenness to touch the lives of others; we are of little use unless we have cried."[74]

Well, let me tell you, I have cried. I have wept, and in fits of anger I have wailed, "Lord, you are expecting too much from me!!" I remember locking myself in my fifth child's nursery room, which was really a converted closet, and screaming at the top of my lungs and with all my soul, "LORD! I am tired—soooo tired. Please, Lord. Please, I can't do it, any of it, all of it, any longer. I quit!" I locked myself in there hoping the older kids wouldn't hear me, but I have the embarrassed notion that strangers on the far side of town probably heard me loud and clear.

More than one time in my life I have felt that God must hate me to have allowed such mind-altering exhaustion. Looking back, however, I understand the good of my eleven-year fatigue. I was becoming useful in the way that Kathleen described as becoming "real." God had given me the opportunity to reorder my life, and in so doing, to become a better mother to my children, a more balanced person myself, and a wounded healer to other mothers whose boats had been simultaneously capsized and set adrift like my own. God is always faithful and as many times as I have quit motherhood, God has let me sit on the bench for a minute, refreshed me with a quick drink, and put me right back in the game.

Being on God's team, I have learned that in the realm of the physical realities of mothering (realities like: the kids have to be bathed, homework has to be done, and bills have to be paid) there are essentially three elements of control at my disposal: time, space, and money. How well I learned to manage these three resources determined my ability to rein in the chaos of childrearing and recover a sense of steering my boat rather than spiraling haphazardly at the whim of passing currents.

Becoming Disciplined

More important for a mother than any methodological systems of time use or space organization or financial budgeting is a theoretically consistent approach to controlling these elements, so that they don't end up controlling her. The foundational aspect of the ability to use time, space, and money skillfully as the raw materials of mothering is summed up in a wonderful little booklet titled *Gathering at the Table* by Elizabeth Hoffman Reed. Acknowledging that celebrating meals together regularly is not an easy thing to do in our activity-obsessed society, Reed encourages us to make it a habit in this way:

> Discipline has a bad name to many people, implying drudgery, rigidity and even punishment. But discipline can offer a framework, a foundation, a path. Think of a person who takes a walk every morning. Knowing that moderate exercise is good for her, she has made a decision to incorporate it into her daily life. So she walks every morning. It is a ritual. She doesn't have to figure out what to do for exercise every day and how to fit it into her schedule. The discipline of the daily walk helps her live out her decision.[75]

Discipline is the master key to accessing and maintaining peace with the physical demands of motherhood. You must *desire the discipline to live out your decision* to be a home-based, family-centered mother. To (1) know God's will (Chapter 2), and (2) prayerfully seek God's call (Chapter 3), I now add (3) discipline to the equation of making peace with motherhood.

Figure 2 is the same photograph of Nicole balancing on a log fallen over the water that I used in Chapter 5, but in this figure I have placed the three *physical* constraints of mothering (time, space, and money) on the forward-moving triangle that represents a peaceful balance. In any given mothering situation you can "shift your weight" among the three points. In other words, if you have more time than money you can make Christmas presents instead of buying them. If you have more money than time, you can buy them. If you have more space than time, you can pick up possible presents on an ongoing basis and store them until the appropriate occasion arrives. All three elements—time, space, and money—are interwoven. In

Photograph by Heidi Bratton.

Figure 2, Physical constraints

order to peacefully maintain your mothering balance and keep moving forward, you need to offset the elements you do not have with the elements you do have.

Please remember that you will need to apply the spiritual virtues from Figure 1 in Chapter 5 (initiative, contentment, and faithfulness) to all of the physical constraints, in order to avoid the pitfall of wanting to have it all and to have it all right now!

Time

Ask any mother who has a child in school what time school begins, even one who educates her child at home, and she will be able to tell you. Seven, eight, or even nine o'clock. Ask the same mother what time her day as a mother begins and she will probably fall on the floor laughing. "The days and nights all blend together with an occasional pause for sleep," she might poetically, if not satirically, answer on a good day. On a bad day she might quip back at you, "Begin? Who cares? I want to know if it is ever going to end? As far as I can remember motherhood started with morning sickness and I haven't had a minute off since!"

Is it any wonder, then, that it is nearly impossible for a mother of young children to hear and understand the wise counsel of a grandmother who comes over to coochy-coo her screaming baby in a checkout line, calmly admonishing the hassled mother to "enjoy these years"? Learning to appreciate the now, to live life in its season, is a difficult task in our fast-paced society. When it comes to time, two things are true: (1) we are all given the same twenty-four hours in a day, and (2) it is never enough. My father-in-law has often quoted Ecclesiastes 3:1 to me in frenzied times of change: "There is a time for everything and a season for every activity under heaven."

Time management tip number one from Ecclesiastes: slow down! Live life in its season. As a society obsessed with motion, we often fail to even consider this as a possibility. "Come on, admit it," encouraged a recent *Reader's Digest* article on time, "you like living at breakneck speed. These days it is possible to drive, eat, listen to a book and talk on the phone—all at once, if you dare."[76] If you are a mom, you can also entertain and feed screaming children in the back seat.

We need to slow down. If we are always rushing about getting the children to all the activities in which they "need" to participate, then we have cheated them out of one critical thing: time to be kids. Time to build blanket forts, dig in the dirt, and imagine that they are Robin Hood. Time to let their imaginations run wild.

Planned Boredom

I am a huge advocate of two seemingly opposite ideas. The first is that a family functions best on structured time or with a schedule. The second is that kids need unscheduled or unstructured time. How do these two ideas coexist? I "schedule" unscheduled time. That is to say, I purposefully plan times when the kids' activities are limited only by their own imaginations. The TV is off. No computer games. Reading is limited. Mom is off entertainment duty except to offer casual suggestions for activities. The great outdoors is wide open. There are siblings, sticks, sand, snow, and a wide assortment of craft materials (minus paint for the pre-schoolers. I'm not completely insane!).

My driving motivation in scheduling unscheduled time is that I believe that boredom is a good thing. In an article titled "In Defense of Boredom" in *Offspring* magazine, parenting educator Carol Kaplan-Lyss says, "Boredom produces a lull that suddenly energizes inner resources."[77] In this same article, Ester Schaler Buchholz, author of *The Call of Solitude*, adds, "Boredom is really just a step before creativity."[78] This is important information for moms who are interested in cutting back on organized activities in order to give their children a more bountiful childhood. Do not be afraid of "I'm bored." On the other hand, understand that unscheduled time is very different than neglecting your children or becoming too busy to interact with them. Unscheduled time is a calculated liberty that gives your child time to hear the beat of his own drum.

Mary Manz Simon gives some prudent advice to one mom struggling to get off the "activity merry-go-round" in her "Ask Dr. Mary" advice column in *Christian Parenting Today*. "In your well-intentioned attempt to stimulate your children and offer enrichment, you may reach a point where you're stuck in schedule gridlock," Simon warns. The time management help Simon offers time-stressed parents and kids is to consider jumping off the merry-go-round. "But be aware," Dr. Mary cautions, "slowing down will be an adjustment for your children. Children who have been highly scheduled go through a transition as they learn how to organize free time, use their imagination and creativity and compensate for boredom."[79]

A Schedule

Of course, planning for unstructured time assumes that you have a plan of how to use your time, or a schedule. A schedule of activities and events is the front line of defense against time stress. No home-based, family-centered mom can afford to be without a schedule. As Reed encourages in her booklet on the benefit of sharing family meals, a schedule is really just a discipline tool to help you live out your decision to take charge of your family's time so that it doesn't take charge of you.

Plan mealtimes. Have an actual bedtime for young children supported by bedtime rituals (e.g., bath, reading stories, brushing teeth) that forewarns the kids of the upcoming event. Have a curfew for older children. My most heartfelt recommendation for family activities to schedule into the daily routine comes from author Gladys

Hunt in *Honey for a Child's Heart: The Imaginative Use of Books in Family Life*. She writes:

> Plan a regular read-aloud time with your child. Few activities are as rewarding as this in creating a warm relationship. There is a good feeling in sharing a story at any age. Children who are read to from the very first come to expect that a book brings pleasure, that letters make words, that words put together in the right way say something that is fun.[80]

It wasn't until after our third child was born that we began to schedule time to read together as a family. But boy, when we did, it took on a life of its own. Today all five kids, toddler to preteen, will rush to get in their pajamas just to hear one more chapter of *Little House on the Prairie*, or of one more hilarious invention in *Homer Price*, before being tucked under the covers. We've even come to treasure long car trips for the time it creates for us to read together.

"We must do more than live in the same house with our children," encourages Gladys Hunt. "We need to spend time with them, talk to them, share our lives with them and teach them. Influencing our children is not a casual task. It won't get done unless we have a plan."[81]

There are so many activities that, although not urgent, are important to building a strong family. Spend your time wisely. Take a regular date night with your spouse. Keep the Sabbath. Schedule unscheduled time and *don't* schedule over it when someone calls and asks if you are busy. Yes, you are busy. You are busy learning how to ease off and enjoy your season with children!

Quantity Time

By now most mothers have realized the ridiculous claim of "quality time" being a sufficient substitute for quantity time. The *Minneapolis Star Tribune* ran a special feature article in its *USA*

Weekend section titled "What Women Want Now." Referencing an opinion poll called "Update: Women," the article noted a dramatic drop (40% in 1998, down from 66% in 1979) in the number of women who agreed with the statement: "It's not the quantity of time you spend with your children—it's the quality."

"While late-70s women minted the concept [of quality time] as a justification for spending less time at home," researcher Laurie Ashcraft explains in the article, "by now many women have decided 'it just doesn't work for them or their kids.'"[82] More and more, mothers are realizing that when it comes to quantity and quality, it is not an either/or scenario. Quantity is as important as quality. You can't expect a child, no matter what age, to disclose all of her concerns, worries, hopes, and dreams to you in fifteen minutes squeezed between activities. A good relationship needs a time-intensive commitment.

Quality Time

On the other hand, I have discovered that by infusing my children with a megadose of concentrated mother-love (by being completely available and intensely present to them for a short period), I can significantly improve their attitudes and create a positive atmosphere in our home that will sustain them through periods when I cannot give them my undivided attention. This is essentially the idea of "quality time" and it works, as long as it is not the only type of time and attention the children get each day. For our family there are five short, critical, quality-time periods in every day. These periods come at times when we are either reconvening after being apart, or going in separate directions after being together: (1) first thing in the morning (I call this period *Greet the Day*), (2) off to school or work or play (*Meet the Day*), (3) after school or naps (*Embrace the Day*), (4) dinnertime (*Discuss the Day*), and (5) bedtime (*Close the Day*). No matter what else I am doing (volunteering in the school classrooms, working on a photography project, or cleaning the house), my goal is to be completely present to the kids at all five of these critical junctures every day.

Basically what I am doing is called "starting off on the right foot," "making a good first impression," or "parting on a good note." The lasting value of these injections of love and attention cannot be underestimated. Dr. James Dobson writes in his book *Life on the Edge,* "When we have been apart from those we love, we have an opportunity to reset the mood. It all depends on the first five minutes [of getting back together],"[83] and the last minute of sending each other off, I would add. Perhaps this is why the Hebrew word *Shalom* and the Hawaiian word *Aloha* mean both hello and goodbye, because times of meeting and departing are similarly times for expressing good will, blessing, and affection that determine the mood of a relationship from that time until the next parting or greeting.

A classic example of the impact of the first five minutes is when the kids wake up and I have the opportunity to set the mood for the day by either greeting them with a "roll-over-and-pretend-I-am-still-asleep" hope that they will go away because I am still very tired and have no desire to get up, or greeting them with a sleepy snuggle and a whispered, but sincere "Good morning. What a pleasure to see you here this fine morning." Given these two ways of greeting a new day with my children, the first type of greeting inevitably starts the day off with everyone being crabby, and it is an attitudinal downhill slide from there. By greeting them positively, even if I am tired and attempt to tuck their squirming bodies in bed with me for a few more minutes of sleep, they start off feeling loved and there is still hope for the day.

Be Trustworthy with Your Time

When my son, Benjamin, was two years old, he went through a stage where whenever I would ask him to do something he would look at me very seriously, put up one little pointer finger, and say, "Just one, Mommy. Just one minute." It was very cute until I realized that he was imitating my response to him whenever he asked me to do something for him! By stalling each time he needed me, I was teaching him a very poor lesson in time management and in relationship dynamics.

Our children must know that when we say that we are available, we are in fact available, lest we exasperate them and teach them that our words cannot be trusted. If you say "one minute," then be available in one minute. If you cannot be available in one minute, do your best to tell them exactly how long it will be until you will be available and then be there for them in that time. You cannot expect them to quietly and patiently wait for you to finish a phone call or a conversation for an *indefinite* period of time. (How would a subordinate, a coworker, or a boss at the office react if you indefinitely put them off?) If you want them to learn to keep their side of the bargain (waiting quietly and patiently), then you've got to keep your side (being available in the time limit you set).

Becoming a trustworthy steward of time is an extremely important skill for home-based, family-centered moms, especially those who are running home businesses or home-schooling. Because your activities outside of mothering are taking place at home, there will be times when you will be wearing your business woman hat or teacher hat at home and be unavailable to be the undivided-attention mom. You will have to resist the temptation to put your young children off with another video or another popsicle and squeeze in one more phone call or impromptu lesson. When your work, or teaching time is up, it is up. For your own mental benefit you may want to build in a little bit of "commute time" to switch mental gears from work to family by wrapping up your activities a few minutes before putting your mothering hat back on.

Space

Four months before our first child was born we purchased a house in a quaint New England neighborhood where we knew absolutely nobody. It was the most beautiful home I could have ever imagined owning. Nestled back from the street on a one-plus acre wooded lot with a stream running along the side, I felt like we were swimming in space—with three bedrooms, two baths, an open-concept kitchen, and a living room that ran the width of the house. We even had a two-car garage and an in-ground swimming pool. I mention that the home was in a New England neighborhood because in this one situation the quintessential, keep-to-themselves view of New Englanders held up. After four years of living in that house I still knew only one neighbor—an extremely busy mother of school-aged children who lived across the street and that I knew more by the coming and going of her minivan than the sum of our conversations. (I understand her busyness so much better now that I have school-aged children myself.)

We had a fantastic group of friends from our church when our first two children were born, but the church was thirty-five minutes south of our new house and we were among the first in the group to have children. Physical isolation from other adults, especially mothers from whom to learn the ropes, was a big problem for me during the years we lived in New Hampshire.

Four years and two kids later, when we moved to California so that my husband could go to graduate school, I suddenly found myself in a two-bedroom, one-bath, second-floor, 650-square-foot apartment. The living room was jammed with a futon couch and a chair. The galley kitchen was so small that I could sit on a stool in the middle of it and simultaneously open the refrigerator, turn on the oven, wash the dishes in the sink, and put a load of laundry in the washing machine. The phrase "bursting at the seams" comes to mind when I remember that apartment. It was a far cry from our generous house on a large wooded lot. The space of our home had been cut by about two thirds, and now instead of a lush yard filled with flowers, sticks, and bugs—and bordered by a babbling brook—we had a concrete parking lot on one side of our apartment and a tiny asphalt courtyard filled with dead grass and broken plastic toys on the other side. Did I feel cheated out of space? You'd better believe I did! Then, I went out to the toy-crowded courtyard with my two small children and found that there were people there, right outside our door, from every country in the world just waiting to play, and moms just waiting to talk. What I had given up in space I gained in friendship and it was worth every inch! Not until we moved to that pint-sized apartment among such diverse and wonderful families did I begin to flourish as a mother.

The mothering/life lesson that I learned from this experience is that babies do not *need* to live in houses owned by their parents. Babies need to live in homes—be they apartments, trailers, houses, condos, grass huts, or boats—where their parents are not financially stressed, emotionally drained and, hopefully, where their parents have a support network of family and/or friends to help them learn the ropes of parenting.

During the four years we lived our two-bedroom apartment life in California, we went from having two children to expecting our fifth baby. As you might imagine, I became an ace at efficient space use and organizing kid stuff.

Stuff

There is an amazing array of really neat gizmos for kids. There are, for example, dozens of ways to carry your baby: backpacks, front-packs, The Sling™, umbrollers, double strollers, jogging strollers, hip-belts, and there are, of course, mothers' arms which children always prefer anyway. Similarly, for any need a growing child will have there will be a plethora of stuff to choose from to fill the need.

There is more stuff for children than for any other creature on this planet (except maybe pets)! The problem is that there gets to be too much stuff and it can take up too much space.

On the physical level of stuff, Dr. Mary Manz Simon advises, "Many times, having too many toys isn't a sign of a spoiled child, but rather the result of well-intentioned giving gone too far."[84] If you can't eliminate all the stuff you already have, at least organize it. Stop yourself and others from buying more. Don't let frantic materialism rule your house. Give museum memberships for Christmas. Ask a grandparent to give the gift of their time for a birthday.

A four-year-old girl, Nancy, provided me with the most hilarious testimony of the need to reduce the number of toys we give our children. One time for lunch I had taken her and her two siblings to McDonald's and had *not* ordered Happy Meals®. Looking at his meal and sensing it was incomplete, her six-and-a-half-year-old brother asked, "Where are the toys?" I explained that I didn't think that we needed to collect any more little plastic toys, so I just got the hamburgers and fries by themselves. Hearing this, Nancy promptly assured me, "Oh, don't worry about that! We don't collect them. We lose them." Silly, silly me.

On the theoretical level of stuff, I became a believer in simplicity while living in our little apartment. Keeping kid stuff to a minimum is the best way to increase the space you already have without spending a dime. Don't keep large items "just in case." Share them with other needy families. Don't keep five different toys where one will do. Don't collect priceless items that you can't bear to part with but that your living room shelves could.

On a spiritual level of stuff, simplicity is a basic gospel truth that Christian singer and songwriter, John Michael Talbot, has written about in his book titled *Simplicity*. I quote at length here because his reasoning is so clear and so biblical:

> There is a perverted kind of teaching in churches today...Things become a sign of God's blessing. Possessions somehow authenticate true Christian faith. This of course goes against the essentials of Christ's teaching of gospel poverty and concern for the world's poor. It is a particular insult to Third World Christians who, in spite of their deep faith and suffering, have little to show in the way of wealth as measured by material possessions.
>
> I believe the true approach to poverty and prosperity can be found in John 15:1–2. ["I am the true vine, and my Father is the gardener. He cuts off every branch in me that bears no fruit, while every branch that does bear fruit he prunes so that it will be more fruitful."]...Here, the teachings of Jesus tell us that God desires both to cut back and to increase. He does not desire that people live in poverty, but he also does not wish that people live in an attitude of materialism and gross consumerism. In order to truly prosper in the spirit, God wishes that we prune our lives so that more fruit may be borne.[85]

Simplicity as an authentic lifestyle is very difficult. Our house-to-apartment experience, however, turns out to be a textbook case about which Paul Wachtel writes in his book *The Poverty of Affluence*. "No amount of material things can ever meet the non-material needs formerly met by community [in traditional cultures]."[86] Space and stuff cannot replace love, no matter how much needed or "cool."

Money

Money is the hardest of all of the physical constraints to balance. It is also the hardest to discuss because every individual handles the commodity so differently. In order to exist and persist as single-income families, mothers with whom I have talked have made a wide variety of financial concessions.

"Our first [financial] adjustment was to have only one car," recalls Carrie. "This meant my husband would ride his bike to work each day. Later when we moved [to a more rural area], it meant I was taking him to work each morning and then, most nights, he would get a ride home from a coworker. We were not able to purchase our first home until after our second child was born and then only with financial assistance from family for the down-payment."

"We gave up being able to eat out at restaurants," Susan tells me in a straightforward manner. "McDonald's is a big occasion for us these days."

"We gave up exotic vacations," says Karen.

Stephanie gave up personal comfort. "At seven months pregnant with my first child we moved into a worn-down apartment building in the middle of the city," she recounts. "We felt it would be best for me to stay home, but realized that if I did we could not pay the bills. Then the opportunity to buy a foreclosure apartment came up. Buying it meant we could rent out the apartments for the extra income, but it also meant we would have to live in one of the apartments! Here was a girl who had traveled the world and lived comfortably all her life...and yet the conviction to be at home to raise these precious treasures meant more to me than the external circumstances I needed to face."

Diane gave up something even more intangible. "I worked for five years before we had children," Diane explains. "During that time I had the satisfaction of knowing that I contributed to our finances. Financially my husband and I were equal partners. After we had kids, I quit my job. I did miss the actual income my job brought in, but more than that, I missed, and still miss, sixteen years later, the satisfaction of contributing."

Like these moms, (my husband and) I have made many and differing financial concessions over the years in order to live on a single income. In making these concessions and reframing our financial expectations, our efforts have collected around four basic tactics: (1) limiting the amount of stuff that we acquire (which I've already talked about in the section on simplicity), *especially* the expensive stuff, (2) taking temporary jobs to meet temporary financial over-runs (or to pay for vacations or one-time purchases), (3) becoming as thrifty as possible, and (4) recognizing the legitimacy of accepting help.

Before launching on your mission to reach the end of the month and be able to pay the bills on one income, it's important to acknowledge that developing and maintaining a budget is ground zero, financial priority #1. You've got to know what your income and your outgo are before you can decide which tactics to apply toward improving your overall financial situation: increasing your income, decreasing your outgo, or some of both.

Temporary Employment

As a financial strategy, temporary employment doesn't need very much explaining, but it is important to mention. Over the years and to cover a number of different expenses, I have taken temporary or side jobs: doing family portraits, giving talks, selling my books at conferences, babysitting a neighbor's child during school vacations, and things like that. Once I even answered an ad in the back of a magazine to string beaded earrings, believing that I really could "make $30 to $40 an hour scheduling my own hours and never having to leave home!" (I still have the beautiful gold glass beads, but not a cent to show for my work, because I was hopelessly incompetent at such detailed work.) More often it has been my husband who has worked a second job, teaching a night class at a nearby college or doing some temporary consulting on the side to cover "outside-of-budget" expenses, simply because his earning power is greater than mine.

A couple of times, when my husband's work has required him to be away from home for an extended period of time, we have rented out our apartment or house so that the kids and I could accompany him. It may seem a bit strange, but except for the house cleaning and packing up of personal belongings, it took very little actual "work" for us to earn the ability to travel to these places as a family.

Making Money by Saving Money

Saving money by "promoting thrift as a viable alternative lifestyle"[87] is the cornerstone of Amy Dacyczyn's fantastically practical book, *The Tightwad Gazette*, which is based on her former newsletter of the same name. The newsletter helped me understand that it is possible to increase your spendable income by reducing your expenses rather than by working longer hours (it's tax free, too). Through Dacyczyn's newsletter, I began to understand that buying the newest or the best was not always the smartest, because smart spending doesn't involve overindulgence or feel-good buying that puts the family in debt. Dacyczyn encouraged me (and all her readers) to explore economical alternatives to expensive items like children's birthday parties, food shopping, and gift giving.

Because of Dacyczyn's publications, I was able to count living in a very small apartment with an extra large family as a blessing rather than a curse. Although I can't claim that I enjoyed it, I counted using cloth diapers instead of disposable ones as a blessing for a few years because a friend donated her entire collection to us after her youngest was potty trained. With between two and three kids in diapers at the same time, using cloth diapers meant hundreds of dollars in savings. Canceling all magazine subscriptions and never signing up for cable TV wasn't so difficult after embracing the idea of making money by saving money. I've learned not to apologize for shopping at thrift stores and wearing hand-me-downs. Camping just a couple of hours from home can be (and usually is) an exotic vacation. Basically, the word *thrifty* has become high praise in our home because of

Dacyczyn's treatment of its meaning. Becoming extravagantly thrifty is one of the prices we pay in order to live on a single income.

Accepting Help

Keeping our methodology in mind of living simply, occasionally moonlighting, and consistently being thrifty, I'd like to be able to tell you that my husband and I have pulled ourselves up by our own bootstraps; that we have pursued the American dream and that all of our sacrifices, hard work, and thriftiness has paid off. I'd like to tell you that by now we have reached the "promised land of financial independence." Oh, how I'd like to tell you that because it would make things so neat and tidy. But the truth is far more complex. We've also had a lot of help. A lot.

Take the time we were in graduate school and I took a small job of cutting brownies for a local caterer to earn a little extra money for Christmas. After she picked up the brownies and (apparently) saw our apartment filled to the brim with children, the delightful, German-born caterer decided to bring us food that she had left over after she catered a men's club luncheon each week. *Gourmet* food *delivered* to us every week for nearly a year all because of one brief brownie-cutting job!

Consider the time my sister took our family of six into her home and cared for us when my husband was unemployed and I was on bedrest expecting baby number five. Consider the aid friends have given us in packing and moving so that we did not have to pay a moving company. Consider that we, too, have received help from our parents in purchasing homes and cars, as well as help in paying for braces for the kids and for medical insurance while we were in graduate school. All these things are a part of our financial story as are giving help to others by supporting charities; giving shelter to a friend estranged from his wife; making meals for neighbors in need;

and donating time, money, and food to the needy wherever we have lived.

"When I was on bed rest with our first child, I was embarrassed to accept all the help friends and family were offering," acknowledges Karen. "Before that time I was always the one helping others. It was a very uncomfortable feeling to have people bringing over dinner and stuff like that. At some point, though, I realized that it wasn't fair to my husband for me to say no to their help. He was the one who would have to come home after a long day at the office and make his own dinner because I was too proud to accept help. So I changed my attitude and said, 'Bring it on!'"

Accepting help is not easy. It did not come any more easily to my husband and me, than it did to Karen. We really fought it in the beginning, believing that we had somehow failed if we admitted needing help of any type. We understand now, having been a part of the full circle of giving and receiving help, that we had not failed, but that God was providing for us through others; the Body of Christ was at work. The best part of being a part of this circle of giving and getting help is our improved ability to help others in a gracious manner that does not impose, threaten, or make them feel indebted—or as if they must have failed or done something to "deserve" being in need.

What I am getting at by examining creative ways of saving and making money *and* encouraging you to both give and receive help, is that in order to take a complete inventory of God's financial provision for your family, you have to look at more than just cash flow. There are more non-monetary than monetary riches that economically sustain our family of seven, and I know that the same goes for most families. God's most amazing provisions don't even show up in the budget. In making the choice to be a home-based and family-centered mom, which probably means living on a smaller family income base, you will benefit from drawing a large circle, one inclusive of God's non-monetary provisions, around your financial picture. Learning to change our perspectives on money brings us to the topic of why women work after they have children.

Why Moms Work

There is a wide range of reasons that a mother may give to explain why she "needs to work." According to Danielle Crittenden in her book *What Our Mothers Didn't Tell Us*, published in 1999, 65 percent of all mothers with preschool age children are in the work force.[88] When asked why this is, many (full-time) working mothers I know simply shrug their shoulders and say, "Hey, what can I do. It's the economy." Honestly, yes, there are mothers in the workplace who are there out of economic need, but still they place their children's needs above their own without any trace of martyrdom, just a steadfast knowledge of their economic situation. As mentioned in Chapter 3, these women, mothers who work out of *true* economic need, not just to pay for a bigger house or a more glamorous vacation or more trendy clothes, are not enemies of the family. But I don't think that the overruling reason why 65 percent of all mothers with preschoolers work is as simple as economics.

Several commentators researching today's cultural norms have turned up other reasons for this trend that have little to do with money. Crittenden, for example, believes that "the fundamental reason mothers of small children feel they can't afford to stay at home, when a generation ago they didn't, is the greater prospect of divorce. The fear a woman has of having to fend for herself and her children at some point underlies why even happily married women often feel obliged to work when there's no immediate financial reason for them to do so."[89]

Dr. Laura Schlessinger, author of *Parenthood by Proxy*, believes mothers work, even when they know it is detrimental to their children,

because of the increasing need among women for occupational identity and self-worth.[90] Arlie Hochschild, author of *The Time Bind*,
believes that the depreciation of home life and the devaluation of
parenting are causing mothers to abandon their children to childcare
workers.[91] Dr. Brenda Hunter, in her book *Home by Choice*, suggests
that women reject a traditional mothering lifestyle (staying close by to
raise their children) because of identification with their fathers'
careerism and for want of his approval. Hunter suggests that this identification with fathers in women stems from fathers who "disparaged
their wives as role models for their daughters,"[92] hindering a close bond
between mother and daughter that may already be strained as the
daughter becomes her own person. Hunter adds that "in the case of
homes marked by marital strife, both parents may have encouraged
their daughters to experience life in ways their mothers had not,"[93] trying to redeem their happiness through that of their daughters.

None of these authors mention money as more than a superficial
reason for so many mothers of preschoolers to be working in the
United States, the most prosperous nation in the world at the beginning of the twenty-first century. I agree with all the authors I've cited
here, but I think that in her book, *Can Motherhood Survive?* Connie
Marshner gets to the absolute core of why so many of today's mothers work outside the home, even when they have young children:

> The cost of having children—*or the fear of the cost*—is scaring women
> away from motherhood or driving mothers out of the home. Fifty years
> ago people didn't feel they had to have air-conditioned houses before
> they could have children. They felt no obligation even to have separate
> beds for children, let alone separate bedrooms! We forget that before
> the post-World War II era of affluence and low interest, it wasn't even
> typical for young families to be homeowners.[94]

"Today, the average house is larger and better, products like TV
sets, stereos, and furniture are cheaper, fresh food is more widely

available," writes Danielle Crittenden, agreeing with Marshner. "Yes, we expect a lot more material comfort nowadays and there are parents who achieve affluence by sacrificing their children."[95]

Basically, we are expecting too much, and we are right back in Chapter 1 trying to decipher why we are expecting to have and to do it all at once. Because of all these combined expectations, there is a perception out there that mothering full time is not an option. It is really a deception behind which we are hiding. We can remain involved in activities we are passionate about without losing our identity (Chapter 2), or having to work at them full time and/or for money (Chapter 3). Fears, not facts, about money, about the prospect of divorce, about the derailing of a career, or about a life of material poverty are driving 65 percent of mothers away from their preschoolers. Financial advisor Larry Burkett put the icing on the cake in his book *Women Leaving the Work Place*:

> The sad truth is that most working mothers sacrifice time with their children with little or nothing to show for it. Most of the average working mother's pay is consumed by taxes, transportation, child-care costs, and clothing. Even when a working mother's income is large enough to substantially add to the family's budget, the surplus is often consumed by an expanded lifestyle.[96]

Choosing to be a Home-Based Mom Is Not a Luxury of the Rich

Program hosts of financial radio talk shows are great at making callers own up to the consequences of their own choices. A caller will phone in with a question about how to get out of debt and the host, after asking a few questions, will say something really simple like "Stop spending," or "Sell your expensive car," or "Don't go on your luxury, time-share vacation this year." The program host always advises the caller to do the obvious thing that he or she doesn't want to hear. Choosing to live on a single income can be similar. We need to own up to the financial choices we have made (large houses, expensive hobbies, feeding our responsibility identities, and so on) that are the real reasons we are working and realize that we should sacrifice these things before we sacrifice time with our children.

Having had five children in rapid succession, I can tell you that our family definitely "needed" a second income, yet we (my husband and I) "chose" that I would not work full time out of the house. What do I mean? Simply that we are the ones who also "chose" to have five children. We were also the ones who "chose" to have my husband go back to school in the middle of having children, which put a huge financial stress on the family. How could we then say that we had no choice—that I "needed" to work outside the home due to the financial burden of so many children and my husband's being in school? It would be a lie. The real choice was not about working, but about how many children to have and if we could afford for my husband to go to graduate school.

I have a great deal of respect for a mother who is working out of true financial need: a mother with older children who is working to pay for their school tuition, or going back to school to finish her college degree, or is engaged in any noble activity suited to her family situation. I hold in highest esteem the mother who is making sacrifices on every front in order to be with her children, especially when they are infants and preschoolers. And, funny as it may seem, I also respect a mother who honestly admits that she is working full time because she likes to work more than she likes to be with her children. I disagree with her choice and its consequences, but I respect her because she is not a hypocrite, hiding behind the mask of affordability.

I once had a conversation with a mom who was hiding behind such an affordability mask. This mom was *not* interested in being at home with her children, but wouldn't admit it. "How nice that you can *afford* to stay at home with your children," said this woman, excusing herself at my expense. "I'd stay home, too…" (long sigh punctuating the inevitable) "if I could." I can't *afford* to be at home either in the way that this mother was using the word to imply that we must be really rich. Such insincerity insulted the sacrificial choices my husband and I (and many other families) make to allow me to be with our children. It also belied the woman's heart and revealed her condescending view of the work of raising children.

The truth? Not all, but many moms (more than 35 percent), some way, somehow, with a little planning, discipline, and help, can be with their children for a few years while the children are young. Raising children is not a luxury of the rich. It is more a matter of choice than we want to admit. When I am confronted with the "I-have-no-choice" attitude, I look to the dire situations of others around me—much worse than I have ever experienced—and I know that choice exists. I hang onto conversations I've had with moms like Stephanie, Susan, Karen, and Carrie, who were willing to gave up "biggies" like cars, eating out, vacations, and single-family houses; moms like Diane, who gave up the satisfaction that comes along with "bringing home the bacon" in order to be there for her kids. It may not always be financially *pleasant* to have one bread-winner in the family, but it seems that it is financially *possible*. Using the tactics I mentioned here, we've succeeded for nearly twelve years. So far, so good.

The Benefits of Living on One Income

The biggest, most significant benefit of choosing to live on one income is for one parent (usually mother) to be able to give adequate time and attention to raising the children. No other benefit comes close to this one in terms of importance or lasting value. However, there is more. For many women an additional benefit is the ability to pursue non-money-making interests like volunteering in the community, home-schooling, or going back to school themselves—the types of activities discussed in Chapter 3.

Carrie, the mother who earlier shared about choosing to have only one car in order to be able to be with her children, comments: "All of our financial choices have and continue to have huge benefits. I am home with my twin two-year-old boys. We spend hours in the backyard digging in the garden, swinging on the swings, reading books, and all the other things two-year-olds enjoy. I see both my girls on and off the bus. I am able to volunteer in the schools my girls attend. I can, on the spur of the moment, pick my oldest up from the bus stop and go sledding with all four kids on a Friday afternoon. I can spend my summers on the beach down the road with the kids."

Karen, the mother who gave up exotic vacations, says "I have gained family sanity (that is, someone who can take care of the house, groceries, errands and all those little things that come up during the week instead of trying to do them on weeknights and weekends). I have also gained more time to be with my husband and child."

Carrie understands that eating at restaurants is a luxury, not an entitlement, and she is willing to trade it for time with her children.

For me, one of the chief benefits of our family's choosing to live on a single income is my ability to pursue my personal goal of being a professional photographer. Because we had already chosen to live on one income, when I decided that I wanted to write and photo-illustrate children's books (a very flexible, but non-lucrative career), I did not have to work overtime in order to earn a promotion or move locations in order to take a higher-paying position. By choice, my photography business is based in my home and grants right-of-way to my children's needs and to my husband's job, but it is not parked and abandoned on the side of the road. As I have practiced my craft at a persistent, tortoise-like pace, I have had the emotional and financial reward of seeing photographs get published and the satisfaction that I have not had to unnecessarily compromise on the care of my children in doing so.

God blesses us when we make good choices. The Contemporary English Version of 2 Timothy 1:7 reads like this: "God's Spirit doesn't make cowards out of us. The Spirit gives us power, love, and self-control." Don't cower under the spirit of fear when you are making family/work choices. Step out in power and love. Remember, there is an element of choice in every situation. Go for the blessing. Use your Spirit-given self-control to save money so that you can buy back as much time as possible with your children.

Should you ever waver in your conviction to use your time, space, and money for the benefit of your family, read Proverbs 10 and 11. Here are just a few encouraging nuggets that they contain: "The LORD does not let the righteous go hungry; blessings crown the head of the righteous; the memory of the righteous will be a blessing; the [wo]man of integrity walks securely; the wages of the righteous bring them life; [s]he who heeds discipline shows the way to life; the lips of the righteous nourish many; the prospect of the righteous is joy; the way of the LORD is a refuge for the righteous; a kindhearted woman gains respect; the desire of the righteous ends only in good; whoever trusts in [her] riches will fall; and the fruit of the righteous is a tree of life."

Focus Questions for Making Peace

1. Which element of life do you see as the biggest obstacle to becoming and remaining home-based and family-centered: time, space, or money? Why? Is there something other than these three standing in your way? What is it?

2. Read Philippians 4:12. How could you compensate for this obstacle by offsetting it with one or both of the other elements?

3. Read Matthew 6:19–34. How could you reduce your dependency on, or minimize the limiting nature of this obstacle?

4. List some of the non-monetary ways that God has provided for your family. Pray for the ability to see the fullness of God's earthly provision for your family and to be grateful for it.

Chapter 7

Romance and Respect: Spouse Support

Marriage takes work. Who knew? Certainly not me when I gleefully accepted a romantic proposal from my lovable hunk twelve years ago. And then there are those precious seedlings, our five children, that are the result of that romantic proposal and gleeful acceptance. More work! Not just for me as the mother or for him as the father, but for us as a couple. In the midst of all the work of parenthood it is easy for a mom to let romance with her spouse wither on the vine.

There was nothing practical or levelheaded about how I found romance or fell in love with my husband. When I first laid eyes on him he was dressed as a clown—literally! The night we met, he and a good buddy of his were dressed in baggy clown suits and rainbow wigs, and were chattering like a pair of squirrels to attract attention and donations for a local water-ski club to which they belonged.

That evening, cool breezes and a faint smell of outboard exhaust floated off the water near the ski dock of the Min-Aqua Bats' clubhouse in the northernmost part of Wisconsin where I grew up. I was there doing a feature article on the water-ski club as a photojournalist for the local newspaper. I zoomed in on this funny boy with my large telephoto lens, and was enchanted by his sky-blue eyes twinkling back at me. Trying to be serious, I snapped a few pictures of him for the article. I was, after all, reporting on a recreational news story of profound importance to all tourists converging on our area in need of entertainment. Really, I was.

With his gaily-colored gaudy figure ironically framed by the serene beauty of a peach and champagne sunset, I saw something I needed in those twinkling eyes under that rainbow wig—fun. I don't want to say that it was exactly love at first sight, I was too sensible for that, but there was this butterfly feeling in my stomach that would not go away. After the ski show I went into the newspaper office, dropped my film off to be developed, jotted a few notes for the article—including a reminder to be sure to use the photo of that clown boy—and went home.

His name was John and he had suggested that he might be out at a favorite local dancing spot that evening and, well, I was smitten enough to go, even though he hadn't exactly asked me out on a date. I dragged my dear sister, Wendy, with me for moral support. ("You have to come with me!" I pleaded, getting her out of bed. "What if I go there and he doesn't even talk to me?") A half hour after my sister and I arrived, I completely abandoned her when John asked me to dance. We danced for about two hours straight—which my sister had suspected we would—but she had been game enough to humor my nervousness and come along anyway.

Still, it wasn't until the evening was over and John offered me a ride home that I fell captive to his charms. Stepping out of the steaming hot dance hall into the blissfully cool summer night he led me over to a baby blue mustang convertible. That was it. I, who had never cared a whit about cars, was in love. He had a terrifically fun personality *and* a totally fun car that matched the color of his eyes. I'd have married him right there.

Now that you know the beginning of our love story, let me give you "the rest of the story," as Paul Harvey would say. The short version is that on that sweet summer night when we met and fell in love, we were both only eighteen and thank God our parents made us go to college! Four years after we met, almost to the day, we were married. For three of those years we dated long distance while he went to college on the East Coast and I in the Midwest. What transpired in those years is what really holds us together. Fun, romance, and adventure remain in our relationship to this day, but it is our shared faith in God that is the glue.

A Shared Faith in Jesus

Marriage is God's provision for the conception and care of children, as well as for companionship for a couple who symbolically become one flesh in the joining of their lives.[97] Even with advances in modern reproductive medicine, women don't get babies without men. Every child has a father. As part of making peace with motherhood, we have to make peace with our children's fathers. Our children's fathers are more than just live-in baby-sitters or disposable influences on our children. Fathers are the very image of our invisible God.

Stephanie and Richard's love story is an ideal Christian love story. Before they met and married, both were strong, convicted Christians. "We both attended a Christian college," recounts Stephanie, "so that before we were even married we had a foundation firmly rooted in Scripture and practical teachings of our faith. This helped us immensely, since we knew basic strategies to decrease tension in the task of parenthood."

"Having Christ in common gives us one less thing to argue about," admits Maria. "Specifically it helped in making difficult choices like where to send the kids to school. We both agreed, despite the cost, that Christian-focused schooling for the kids was our number one priority. We've encountered many difficult decisions like that where our faith has given us common ground."

Not all couples, however, start off equally yoked. My husband, for instance, had a relationship with the Lord before we met. I did not. I grew up in the church, but my husband was the first person to introduce me to Jesus as Savior and Friend. John lived his life differently because of his faith and as our relationship grew, it was John's God that became even more attractive to me than his sky-blue eyes or his matching convertible. I gave my life to the Lord a year after we met and was filled with a profound sense of coming home. Awakening to God's love for me as an adult, becoming a true believer, was the fulfillment of everything that I had been taught in church every Sunday and by my parents every day of the week. It just took me awhile to really understand.

I can't say if my husband would have still married me if I had not come to know the Lord, or even if our marriage would have survived under those conditions. But I can tell you that in many situations we've faced since saying "I do," it has been God's grace, not the good will or good intentions of either John or me, which has kept us happily married. Even if your husband does not share your faith, you need to invite Jesus to be in your marriage. If the Holy Spirit is alive in your life, then faith can be a part of your marriage.

Romance and Respect

"Throughout all time, little girls have looked to marriage as the culmination of all of one's hopes and dreams," confesses Susan Alexander Yates, author of *And Then I Had Kids*. "Herein lies the problem. In reality when we say 'I do,' we are committing ourselves anew to work at the relationship."[98] When we marry we are committing to the permanency of our relationship with our spouse and that permanency is going to take more than romance. It's not that God's grace isn't sufficient; it is. But we're the ones, husband and wife, that said "I do."

Committing myself to work at our marriage has not always been easy. I am extremely driven. My husband has a much more passive approach to life. I am inexhaustibly communicative. He is not. I'm an organization freak. He is an absent-minded professor. My motto is "Just *do something*—sit, stand, or get out of the way!" His motto is "It will be there tomorrow." We've both toiled a bit with understanding and respecting our polarized personalities. We've had some pretty chilling conflicts as a result of living under the same roof and trying to raise children together.

The point is, I romantically *fell in love* with this really cute guy with a really cool car, but I choose daily to *be in love* with the same guy who now drives a used Escort wagon with 127,000 miles on the odometer and a few dings on the side door. Some days our marriage relationship is as natural as falling off a log. Other days it is anything but natural to pull myself away from the children, the home, and my photography/writing in order to reconnect with my husband. Love is both a *feeling* and a *decision*.

Dr. James Dobson wrote in his June 2000 newsletter to *Focus on the Family* constituents, "The critical element [in divorce] is the way a husband or wife begins to devalue the other and their lives together. It is a subtle thing at first, often occurring without either partner being aware of the slippage.... If there is hope for dying marriages, and I certainly believe there is, then it is likely to be found in reconstruction of respect between warring husbands and wives."[99] In marriage each partner needs to be forgiving, to be tolerant of non-essential differences, to continue courting the other's affections, and to be secure as an individual. Maria Shriver writes in her book, *Ten Things I Wish I'd Known Before I Went Out into the Real World*, that her husband, Arnold Schwarzenegger, told her even before they were married not to expect or rely on him to make her happy. "You must be happy with yourself first. Be happy with your life separate from what the other person brings to the table."[100] The truth is that we cannot live vicariously through our spouses. Love will fade unless respect is cultivated just as romance is stoked between partners.

Taking the importance of marriage one step further, Marian Wright Edelman believes that the process of reconstructing a failing marriage is our duty to our children. In her book, *Lanterns: A Memoir of Mentors*, Edelman shows no tolerance for the self-seeking style of marriage that has brought our country to a fifty percent divorce rate:

> Keep your word and your commitments. If you get married, stay married. Your children need stability and marriage is not to be shed lightly like old clothes. While I do not condone tolerating domestic violence or conditions where it is unsafe for a spouse or a child to remain in a family, I also do not believe that simply seeking personal happiness or fulfillment should come at the expense of a child's home and well being. Who among us has not been bored, angry, disappointed, or eager for a more exciting and fulfilling spouse—sentiments I'm sure our spouses have shared. But a family is more than the desires of one or both adults. Children should come first.[101]

While I completely agree with Edelman, I believe that the only way to prevent a marriage from becoming an empty, barely-working relationship between near strangers that inevitably dissolves when the children leave home, is to understand that tending to our marriage comes even before tending to our children. It is easy to get trapped in the manipulative game of who needs mom more—husband or kids? Obviously a baby places life-sustaining demands on mom, but a wife should no more use these demands as convenient excuses to brush her husband aside than a husband should bulldog his way back into center stage, not allowing for his wife's multifaceted distraction.

As easy as it is to lose romance and joy in the midst of all the work of raising a family, it is important to maintaining peace with motherhood that you foster intimacy with your spouse, keeping the flame alive. Your marriage relationship is the foundation of your family, a springboard to joy and companionship, a cushion of fellowship and solace in motherhood. Too many women (and men) today regard their marriage vows and their mystical oneness in Christ as throwaways. A wedding becomes a mere rubber-stamping ceremony of a transitory alliance between partners who shared sexual intimacy long before. Forgetting even this perverse grip of the reality that denies the ongoing pain of divorce, for your own sake, completely independent of the children (and yet for their sake, too), forging a good marriage is well worth the sweat.

His Work and My Work

If we want to *have* the best spouses in the world, we need to *be* the best spouses in the world. We can't have a double standard about how much hubby should do when he comes home from work and how many breaks mom should get because she has been with the kids all day. The following excerpts are from a 1960 high school Home Economics workbook:

> How to be a Good Wife: Have dinner ready [when your husband gets home from work]: plan ahead, even the night before, to have a delicious meal on time. Prepare yourself: Take fifteen minutes to rest so that you'll be fresh when he arrives [home]. Touch up your makeup, put a ribbon in your hair. He has just been with a lot of work-weary people. Be a little more interesting. His boring day may need a lift. Try to encourage the children to be quiet. Don't complain if he is late for dinner.[102]

I would go on, but fear making every woman ill. Surely the feminist movement has liberated our culture from this barbaric understanding of husband-wife relationships. Or is it truly barbaric? Who among us wouldn't like it if our husband treated us in such a self-sacrificing way after a long and weary day of mothering? Who among us wouldn't respond with gratitude and a renewed willingness to serve our husbands in turn?

Regarding this point, Kathy's story is significant.

Recently, I was thinking about my husband's difficult childhood and the neglect that he and the other kids in his family suffered. It wasn't that his parents were awful or that they didn't love him, it was just that they were struggling with a myriad of problems and they were simply overwhelmed. As a consequence, his parents escaped to work outside the home and the house deteriorated. The kids were embarrassed to bring friends to their home. The bathroom especially was a source of frustration. The sink was full of hair, the tub was rarely clean, and the toilet seat was continually broken. I realized that my own effort to keep a very clean bathroom was my little attempt to somehow heal the brokenness that my husband had experienced long ago. He may never consciously understand this, but I am sure it does make him feel loved by me at the deepest level.

There are two sides to the "How-to-be-a-Good-Spouse" coin. Side one is that husbands should absolutely help out around the house and, more important, with raising the children. Absolutely. Mom should not be left holding the bag on every decision as it relates to the kids. If, as I said before, mom should not regard dad as nothing more than a *live-in baby-sitter*, dad should not look on mom as merely an *unpaid baby-sitter* (and/or housekeeper)! If you feel belittled by your spouse, or believe that he does not hold your contributions to family in very high regard, this is a problem that needs to addressed as soon as possible and with third-party help, if necessary.

The flip side of the coin returns us to Kathy's story. We need to make choices for our marriage that are life-giving, not life-taking. Keeping a scoreboard rarely strengthens a relationship. If your husband is involved and trying to be a good spouse and father, then it is time to drop the shrill party line about oppressive, egalitarian husbands. If you are married, it can only be to one man. If that one man is doing well by you and the family, then count your blessings and stop picking on the guy just because he was born with more testosterone than you were. By developing an abrasive, entitled attitude about hubby's doing "his fair share" of family and household duties, we are not encouraging him to be a self-motivated family player; we are pushing him farther out the door, shooting our motherhood right in the foot.

"I think it is safe to say," comments Danielle Crittenden in *What Our Mothers Didn't Tell Us*, "that there has been no generation of men raised with fewer expectations of what their wives will do for them than this current one."[103] The feminist movement has transformed men's expectations in just about all areas of life. Being a man, a husband, and a father today is very confusing. We expect men to develop all the nurturing qualities of a woman and yet not misplace all their desirable masculine qualities in the process. Returning to Dr. Dobson's advice, we must not devalue our spouses' efforts. We must continually work to build or even to reconstruct respect for their good characteristics.

Sometimes, as in the following stories shared by Jennifer and Stephanie, we women don't realize just how much our husbands are capable of until there is a real need. Jennifer, mother of a one-year-old daughter, tells us:

> I expected to be fully prepared for motherhood in every way, including taking a weekend course in labor and delivery with my husband; purchasing the "essentials" on the lists found in parenting books and magazines (three onesies, two hooded towels, four pairs of socks, two lullaby CDs, and so forth); working out a proposed schedule for feeding, napping (for me too), and grocery shopping; taking a breastfeeding class and a nutrition class; organizing all of our closets; finishing the painting in our living room.... I could go on forever.
>
> What happened is that our four pound bundle of joy arrived eight weeks early without notice. I was out cold for an emergency c-section which we knew very little about. Our house was a mess. I learned breastfeeding on the fly and didn't even get to feed her directly (I was pumping) for the first two weeks. We had no clothing that fit her and ended up shopping in between feedings at the hospital for something for her to wear. We quickly learned to roll with the punches of her schedule since she was not a sound sleeper and rebelled against any schedule or routine we tried to impose upon her. As for the grocery

shopping, our friends and family cooked for us for a while, then my husband took up most of the slack, bringing me nourishment whether or not I was hungry.

When the dust settled, we realized that the most important thing was that we were all healthy and alive. I also learned that I could not have chosen a better advocate and caretaker than my husband. He came through with flying colors in our time of need. Whether it was making sure the nurses were taking good care of me, checking in on our daughter and holding her in the NICU when I was too sick to, calling friends and family, or sleeping next to my hospital bed in an uncomfortable chair, he was there for me 100 percent. We may not have had all of our ducks in a row where organization, training, and material goods were concerned, but we had all we really needed in a healthy daughter and a stronger family than ever.

I am most impressed by one element of Jennifer's story. In writing about her mothering experiences she uses the word "we" more often than "I." To me this indicates a strong and real partnership with her husband in parenthood.

Stephanie shares a similar crisis that allowed her husband to get in on the ground floor of parenting where she may have been tempted to corner the market before he ever had a chance:

My husband was thrust into fatherhood immediately. My own reins of control were useless as I had complications and had to have an emergency blood transfusion after delivery. My husband changed my daughter's first diaper, gave her her first bath...everything. So we became partners in parenthood from the beginning and the bond he shares with all our [four] children is a result of my needing to let go and allow God to work out the logistics of my given predicament.

"For a woman to do effective mothering she needs not only a harmonious marriage, but she also needs for her husband to be emotionally supportive. Any woman who lives in a chaotic marriage without sufficient emotional support cannot possibly devote herself fully to mothering," Dr. Brenda Hunter explains in her book *Home by Choice*.[104]

"We need to be generous, not stingy, with our love for and attention to our husbands' needs. Our generosity will come full circle when they respond by showing genuine respect and support for our aspirations as mothers and as individuals."[105]

Letting Dad Become Dad

So, how do we do this? How do we let dad become Dad, barring some medical crisis like Jennifer and Stephanie experienced? The starting point should be obvious, but many of us women miss the truth that men cannot be mothers. For example, they usually are rougher than moms are, more apt to wrestle than to cuddle with the kids to show their affection. But if wrestling is their show of affection, then it is good. Different, but good. Men can only be fathers, not mothers, and our children *need* them to be fathers. We can certainly help them in becoming fathers, but we won't do it by henpecking them into mirror images of ourselves.

My husband and I came to a point in our parenting where we had to have a real heart-to-heart about both of our expectations of him as a father. He felt that I was always hovering around when he was with the kids, sort of grading his fathering to see if it would measure up to my mothering. I protested that I was only trying to help! I, after all, was with them twenty-four hours a day, seven days a week. Who better to help him out? Our intermittent discussions on the topic went on for several years until I came to the point where I said, "Okay. They are yours. Father away. Only promise me one thing—their safety. Promise me that you will keep them safe and then I will stop hovering." His immediate response was, of course, "Define safety." For which I threw up my hands and let out a good feminist shriek/groan.

135

Becky Tirabassi, author of *Being a Wild, Wacky, Wonderful Woman for God*, describes being at home with her young son as being "as difficult as following a slow tractor on a country road in a no-passing zone."[106] This may be a good word picture for how long it may seem to take your husband to become a good dad and how patient you may need to be while you wait. We begin to know our babies nine months before dad does. We begin to bond through the simple act of nursing. Dad does not have these advantages. Whether motherhood comes perfectly naturally or not, something very deep within our feminine beings prepares us to nurture life. This doesn't happen with dad. But just as it is a worthwhile commitment, for the children's sake, for us to slow down and develop the parenting instincts that do not come naturally to us, it is worthwhile, for the children's sake, for us to stand aside and to let our spouses give parenting a try, too.

A few years ago I had an occasion to share our wedding album with a new friend. As we sat together flipping through the pages I found myself scanning the photographs, almost subconsciously, for the faces of our children, even though I knew they would not be there. I wanted to tell my new friend, and I knew my husband would agree, that "Yes, there we are on our wedding day, but you really can't see the fullness, the fruitfulness of our marriage without looking at this year's photo album. You have to see the kids, too."

Husband and wife, freshly married on their wedding day, are two pristine rose buds, beautifully poised, full of the promise of opening. A rich family life, spilling over with children and vivacious activity, is a whole bouquet of midsummer wildflowers capriciously stuffed in a vase! Do the necessary work to hold onto the incredible flowering joy of your wedding-day promise.

Focus Questions for Making Peace

1. Recall the first time you met your husband. Name one thing that attracted you to him. Will you share this good memory with him?

2. Read Genesis 2:8–25. Dwell on verse 20. How does it make you feel to know that part of the fullness of God's plan for your life as a married woman is to be a suitable helper, an appropriately adapted companion, for your husband?

3. On a scale of 1 to 10 (1 being not very much and 10 being a lot), how involved is your husband with your children? If there were one way you would ask your husband to improve in fatherhood, what would it be? What could you do to encourage and support this improvement? Will you do it?

4. In what one concrete way could your husband better support your dreams and ambitions?

5. In what one concrete way could you better support your husband's dreams and ambitions?

Part III

The Impact of Our Peace

Chapter 8

The Political Impact of Our Peace: Influencing the Social Agenda of Our Culture

When I look at the political influence Christian organizations are having on our contemporary culture and at the steady influence of Christians in secular organizations, I am proud to be a believer. Parachurch organizations like *Focus on the Family*, the *National Right to Life Committee*, the *Family Research Council*, the *Le Leche League*, MOPS (Mothers of Preschoolers, International), *Concerned Women for America*, *Mothers at Home*, and *Hearts at Home* have joined traditional churches in political advocacy for prolife, profamily government policies.

Mothers at Home, an organization of which I am a member, has public policy directors who, according to Dana Mack in *Assault on Parenthood*, "have taken public stands for measures that would promote at-home mothering—including policies that would make home-based employment easier and remove tax incentives for daycare."[107] Looking at the homespun format of their monthly newsletter, *Welcome Home*, I would never have guessed that the moms running *Mothers at Home* were so politically savvy—which makes my point.

Velvet Over Steel

Being home-based, family-centered moms—hands-on and kid-friendly—does not mean that we should be pushovers. In their eloquent book on child discipline, *When You Feel Like Screaming*, Pat Holt and Grace Ketterman paint a "three-word picture of the mother who is fun, loving, fair, gentle, yet exudes strength and control" that I have not forgotten. The phrase they used to describe such a mother is "velvet over steel." The term *velvet* describes what every mother imagines herself to be—soft, fun-loving, kind, loving, and lovable. The term *steel* "gives strength and meaning to every word a mother speaks—she means what she says and says what she means—all of the time," the authors explain. "A velvet-over-steel mother...cannot be worn down or manipulated because she is secure and her child can trust her. The undergirding of strength and control (steel) allows her to be fun-loving with her children and even permits her to act silly (velvet)."[108]

Although coined to help mothers remember how to both enjoy and confidently shape their sometimes boisterous and disobedient children without screaming, the term "velvet-over-steel" reflects my exact image of the directors of *Mothers at Home*. They are neither homebodies that avoid our unwholesome cultural environment in order to provide "a wholesome childhood to beloved children,"[109] nor are they screamers who find fault with everything the government does.

Supporting, Not Defeating, Motherhood with Government Spending

One of the most important things we can do to improve, revolutionize, and support motherhood is to stay on top of, and get involved in, politics that affect the family. Marian Wright Edelman, founder of the Children's Defense Fund, has been a phenomenal force in promoting child-friendly public policy in our nation and in shaping public opinion on the importance of giving sufficient attention to all children. In her book, *The Measure of Our Success*, Edelman writes: "Take parenting and family life seriously and insist that those you work for and who represent you do. Our leaders mouth family values they do not practice. Seventy nations provide medical care and financial assistance to all pregnant women; we aren't one of them. Seventeen industrialized nations have paid maternity leave programs; we are not one of them."[110]

In this book Edelman, a Southern Baptist, quotes this pastoral letter written by the National Conference of Catholic Bishops titled, "Putting Children and Families First: A Challenge for our Church, Nation, and World":

> The most important work to help our children is done quietly—in our homes and neighborhoods, our parishes and community organizations. No government can love a child and no policy can substitute for a family's care, but clearly families can be helped or hurt in their irreplaceable roles. Government can either support or undermine families as they cope with the moral, social, and economic stresses of caring for children.
>
> There has been an unfortunate, unnecessary, and unreal polarization in discussions of the best way to help families. Some emphasize the primary role of moral values and personal responsibility, the sacrifices to be made and the personal behaviors to be avoided, but they often ignore or de-emphasize the broader forces which hurt families, e.g., the impact of economics, discrimination, and antifamily policies. Others emphasize the social and economic forces that undermine families and the responsibility of government to meet human needs, but they often neglect the importance of basic values and personal responsibility (p. 7).[111]

"The undeniable fact," Edelman concludes, "is that our children's future is shaped by both the values of their parents and the policies of our nation."[112]

Soldiers on the Home Front

In *Assault on Parenthood*, Dana Mack describes several government initiatives that "insist that strong, healthy families are integral to a strong, healthy society that has children's well-being at heart"[113] and that encourage women to live life in its season. One, in particular, jumped off the pages of her book at me, screaming of good, common sense with an established precedent:

> Government might also require employers to institute preference-in-hiring policies for parents who are returning to work after a hiatus for child-rearing—the same sort of preference-in-hiring arrangement, indeed, given to veterans who have interrupted participation in the labor force to serve in the armed forces.[114]

That is a beautiful concept! We as a nation have validated the importance of the work of the people who defend our country from outside military threats by instituting preference-in-hiring policies for them when they return from military duty. In 1945 the G.I. Bill of Rights gave every serviceperson discharged from World War II money to pay for books and tuition in order to help them resume the educational opportunities they had lost while serving in the war. Brown University in Rhode Island even created a Veteran's Extension Division (later known as the Veterans College) to help men and women who served in the war "get back up to speed academically."[115]

Can we validate the importance of defending our families, the very foundation of our civilization, by instituting preference-in-hiring policies for women (and men) who "interrupt participation in the labor force" to serve as parents? This is the best political idea I have heard to date. It creates a cultural environment that encourages giving adequate attention to the needs of children and supports a woman's desire to fill those needs herself. It also allows a woman to fulfill personal ambitions by using her gifts and talents outside of the home when she is ready. It says that family and work are not mutually exclusive because they do not have to be accomplished at the same time. Most important, writes Mack, summarizing her thoughts on prudent, family-wise use of public funding, "instead of directing government monies toward increasing child-care options for working parents, our government should engage itself in relieving parents of work pressures and encouraging solutions that maximize family time."[116]

In her most recent book, *Lanterns: A Memoir of Mentors*, Marian Wright Edelman advocates that her readers take a "parent's pledge." Part of this asks a parent to pledge to "speak up and stand up for my children's needs and support effective groups that help children." "You are your child's greatest advocate," she continues. "Use your power to speak and act on their behalf. Our children and families are facing one of the worst crises in American history and we've got to do something about it. Our voices united in concern can make a mighty roar."[117]

Influencing the political, mothering agenda of our culture is one place where I fall far short of my own hopes for involvement. You could probably relate if I simply said, "there just isn't enough time." But this does not let you or me off the hook. If you are not able to participate in any of these outstanding political organizations or to keep track of the many political initiatives affecting your family, as I am many times unable to do, consider making a commitment to do three things: (1) pray for them, (2) support them financially, and (3) vote! To disengage from the political process is to miss the opportunity to set in motion policies that will make it easier for our daughters and sons to make the right choices when they become moms and dads. Leave a legislative legacy.

Focus Questions for Making Peace

1. Would you rather "work fewer hours while raising children and postpone retirement until the age of 70 or work more hours while raising children and be able to retire at age 60"?[118]

(A 1993 *Family Research Council* poll indicated that the majority of Americans would choose the later "retirement strategy of organizing work and family responsibilities over the life cycle." Restructuring government funding in this way, coupled with passing tax-relief proposals and parental leave programs rather than underwriting daycare, would help women (and men) to remain at home with children saving a generation of children from inadequate mothering.)[119]

2. Did you vote in the last election? If not, and if you remember, why not? What would motivate you to take some role in promoting profamily policies?

3. Read 1 Timothy 5:8. How can involvement in politics help provide for your family?

Chapter 9

Our Esteemed Colleague: Winning Respect for Our Choices

One morning while we were living in Berkeley, California—a rare sunny morning between winter rainstorms—I experienced the error of not sharing my schedule, or time boundaries, with a neighbor. A very nice Christian neighbor, who had one three-year-old child, called up and invited my daughter, Olivia, to go on a jaunt to a nearby park. Olivia was eighteen months old at the time and her younger sister, Lucy, was all of three weeks old. It was a wonderful invitation that would allow Olivia to get out of the house for the first time in almost a week and allow me to get the laundry folded and off the bed so that I could nap with the baby before picking up the two older kids from school at 2:45 P.M.

Unfortunately it wasn't until nearly 2:30 P.M., when my Olivia still was not home, that I realized that my neighbor and I had very different understandings of what it meant to "be home by lunch." To flesh out your understanding of the unfolding drama, let me confess that in our family napping is not considered a luxury, but a social responsibility—especially for mommy. Some people consider recycling, conserving water, and saving the whales to be of utmost importance. Not us. While we are as environmentally conscious as the next person, taking a nap, and thereby saving the world (especially the people nearest to us) from contagious and uncontrollable end-of-the-day crabbiness, is understood to be among the most noble societal deeds anyone can perform.

Because my neighbor said she would be back around lunchtime, noonish by my definition, I didn't lie down to nap when baby Lucy fell asleep around 12:30 P.M. I waited, awake, until exhaustion, coupled with fear of not knowing where my daughter was, transformed me into a true viper. I could hardly contain my fury when my neighbor breezed up the stairs to our apartment at 2:30 P.M. with two wearied toddlers in tow and casually knocked on the door. "Oh, we had such a glorious time!" my friend cooed cheerily, totally unaware of my fear and fatigue-induced wrath. "I fed the girls a little snack at the park, but Olivia is probably ready for lunch and a nap by now," she chirped. "I hope you weren't worried, but I thought you wouldn't mind if we were a little late. I figured you could have more time with the baby." I bit my lip, picked up my over-tired little girl, and managed a polite thank-you before ushering my neighbor out the door. Jarring the sleeping baby out of her cradle and into her car seat without having the time to nurse her, and throwing a screaming, hungry Olivia in the back seat beside her sister, I raced through several stop signs trying to get to the older kids' school on time.

I *did* mind. I had been worried. I did *not* get more time with my baby, and now I was late for pick-up time. The situation was an acute reminder of my need to clearly communicate with my colleagues in mothering. I should have simply said, "If she goes with you, Olivia will have to be back by noon. Is that okay with your schedule for the day?" I could have saved myself a big headache. My neighbor could have said "yes" or "no." As it was, she felt she had done me a great favor and I was running around like a rabid dog as a result of her good deed. My failure to articulate my needs was terribly unfair to my neighbor's good will.

Being Frank

So why didn't I talk to her about my schedule? Well, this particular mother and I had incredibly different styles of mothering. We shared common values, but implemented them in totally different ways. I was afraid to ask her to have Olivia home by noon because my neighbor did not believe in keeping kids on a schedule and I was too tired that morning to get into it with her.

This mother's one child was three years old. Because of this she could afford a more free and easy manner about schedules. Her child was older and their activities could be more flexible. I didn't begrudge her this freedom. (I didn't even wear a watch myself until my oldest daughter entered kindergarten and I was scared to death I'd forget to pick her up if I didn't start keeping better track of time.) By the time that I became friends with this neighbor, however, I had just given birth to my fourth baby in six years and the two oldest children had school-imposed schedules of their own. Without scheduled nap times, our household ran the risk of complete ruin. My neighbor's did not. Neither of us was "wrong." We simply had differing mothering demands and different ways of meeting those demands.

Allowing for Imperfection

Up to this point I've shared all about how good choices and self-discipline can help us accomplish our goal of making peace with motherhood. In this chapter I want to throw in the counter-balance: it is impossible to be perfectly peaceful, efficient, planned, organized, and effective at every turn. The English poet and novelist Eugene Lee-Hamilton wrote about a walk through the forest, as follows: "My soul has mingled with the Forest's soul; Danced with its light and shadows; laughed its laugh; Caught every lightest whisper as it stole."[120] The enchanting picture that this poet paints is of a leaf-covered, forest floor dappled with sunlight and shadow. Peace with motherhood is like that dappled forest floor. Peace is found. Peace is lost. We must learn to dance and to laugh and to go along because peace, like sunlight, is not ours to possess. Peace, like love, is both a feeling and a commitment. Peace with motherhood can be a tranquil state of affairs or a resident, inner strength amid times of complete outer turmoil.

Clearly thought-out expectations, realistic boundaries, and workable systems are the tangible tools of peace in home-based, family-centered mothering. But in order for these tools to be effective they must be communicated to and respected by family, friends, and neighbors—in other words, by your colleagues. By "winning respect from your colleagues" I mean that those around you would come to show regard and consideration for the expectations, boundaries, and systems you have developed, even if they do not respect them in the sense of sharing them or even esteeming you for having them.

Winning Respect

The first step toward winning respect for your efforts at peace with motherhood is comprised of the soul-searching we have been discussing up to this point: rethinking your expectations, grounding your self-esteem in Christ, and establishing structure. This can be a tedious step, but you cannot skip over it if you really want to make lasting peace with motherhood. If you have been reading along to this point, but not really allowing the words to penetrate your heart and influence your actions, go back to page one. Or dig out your Bible and begin your own journey with the Lord. Whichever you do, don't skirt around self-evaluation and disdain godly heart examination, because the process holds so much promise for order and peace in your life that it is well worth the effort.

The second step toward winning respect for our mothering choices is being brave enough to share them with our colleagues.

Ideally you will have developed your expectations, boundaries, and systems with the input of family members, so that your family should not only respect but encourage your mothering goals and the boundaries and systems you have put in place to support those goals. If we do not honestly *share* these objectives with our colleagues, we cannot expect them to be respected, just as I really had no right to be angry with my neighbor for bringing my daughter home at 2:30 P.M. instead of at noon.

The third step in winning and maintaining respect for our boundaries and systems is maintaining a flexible attitude when things do not work out. Neighbors are important. I should have had a much kinder opinion of my neighbor for liberating my eighteen-month-old from the house for a day of fun in the sun instead of being so anxious about how much she had inconvenienced me in doing so. Schedules don't *have* to be kept on the one sunny day granted from heaven amid weeks of rain.

Being Flexible

To be completely honest, it is this third step, flexibility, which is the hardest step for me. Try as I might to maintain my boundaries, nature abhors a vacuum (as do cats). Every time I clear some space, set aside some time, or save some money for my home-based business—Wham! the kids need *my* extra desk for a school project, a snow day is called from school on *my* day to work, or the car breaks down and the cost to repair it is the exact amount I have saved for *my* project. Finally, I'm coming to have a sense of humor about this "vacuum principle." I'm learning to stick to the office space, the schedules, and the budgets I have created without getting overly protective or angry every time someone comes up with a different way to fill them.

I have a dear friend and mentor, Mary, who is fifty-four years old. During one of our conversations around the afternoon snack table at my house, and in between interruptions from the kids, she laughingly assured me that this is life! "*This*," she exclaimed, opening her arms and her eyes to encircle the table full of kids and cookie crumbs and to include the chaos of my house in general, "is normal!" She advised me not to sit around waiting for things to settle down and for com-plete peace to be achieved before I pursued "the rest of my life." Mary shared that she had waited, put a few things on hold, believing that certainty and steadfast security were just over the horizon. "But they were *not*," she said. "The thing to do is to just hang on for the ride."

So I admit that as much as I would like to believe that I own and control all the time, space, and money systems I have worked so hard to set up, set aside, and preserve for my activities with my kids, these things are not *mine*. I do not possess the little people I bore any more than I can possess sunlight and peace. Peace with motherhood is not a static condition. Peace is like a mobile. When one of the hanging objects moves, the entire mobile bobs and sways. If we work so hard at keeping everything perfectly still, every boundary in place, we will miss much of the beauty of raising a family. We need to be flexible. We need to create joy and times to enjoy.

Being Fun

Gwen [Weisling] Ellis is the mother of two grown children and an accomplished writer and editor. Her first book, *Raising Kids On Purpose For the Fun of It*, was one of the first books I read as I began my jour-ney toward making peace with motherhood. The title of her book caught my eye immediately. The thought of raising kids *on purpose* suggested choosing to do it, and *for the fun of it* suggested that it could be some sort of an adventure. I was very interested to learn about both of these ideas, especially about how mothering could be an adventure.

As I read Ellis's book I was delighted to hear that in order for par-enting to be a fun adventure, planning was an absolute necessity. I totally and emphatically agree—a peaceful mother needs a plan. Better yet, Ellis continuously emphasized the purpose of a mothering plan: to value experiences over things, time over money, and people over possessions. The intensity of her years spent as a full-time home-maker, purposing a wonderful home for her children, rich in experiences and traditions, is revealed in Ellis's definition of home:

> The four walls you live within are not a home. They are a house. A home is what happens among the people who live inside those four walls. A home is a place where values can be learned as children are encouraged, instructed, and nurtured. A home is a place of sharing, and probably the most important thing you can share there are your values, the fabric of which your child's life will be constructed.[121]

Motherhood did not just happen to Ellis. She did it on purpose. As I have followed her work since that first book, a new theme appeared in her writing: relaxation. This is a quote from *Thriving as a Working Woman*, written six years later: "At some place and time in our lives, we have to finally admit that the world does not revolve around what we do and don't do. No person in indispensable. We have to give ourselves permission to relax—to stop working."[122]

Developing an attitude of fun permeates both of Ellis's books, but in the second one she seemed to have matured past her workaholic, I'm-going-to-make-motherhood-fun-or-else tendencies. We need to have plans and goals but not to lose sight of the purpose of them—the enjoyment of family life. The proverbial saying that we should take time to smell the roses seems to fit here or, as I think of it, we should take time to gather the wildflowers.

Be a Blessing, Not a Curse

We are not at the whim of other people's responses to our motherhood, whether they are degreed experts or just nice neighbors. We can have our own minds about the value of schedules and routines or how to dress and discipline our children. When we are at peace with motherhood, we can even share our mindset with others without threatening or belittling them for their different opinions. It is most often true that we teach others how to treat us by (1) the way we treat them, and (2) the way we react to their treatment of us. Whenever I have the opportunity to respond to a person's negative reaction toward me as a mother, or toward motherhood in general, or if I find myself afraid to tell someone something with which I know they will disagree, I find strength in a verse from Psalm 118:26: "Blessed is (s)he who comes in the name of the Lord."

I can be a blessing to someone—a ray of sunshine piercing though a dreary day in March—if I will only be brave enough to speak the truth of my convictions about motherhood in love, perhaps even in the face of hurtful, demeaning, or simply oblivious remarks. It is hard to do. Very hard to do. But I remember a time of airing doubts about mothering to my friend, Kathleen, with status-quo negativism and gloomy despondence, only to be blessed by her. In the face of my consolation-prize "aw" about the situation, Kathleen chose to respond with a cathedral-entrance "ah" and say, "Yes, the situation is tough. But, not only is it worth the trouble, I know you can do it!" My friend's positive response taught me how to treat her and how to discuss motherhood in her presence. Instead of joining in my cursing, she began blessing.

Marian Wright Edelman says it nice and succinctly in Life Lesson 16 of her book, *Lanterns: A Memoir of Mentors:*

> Be real. Try to do what you say and say what you mean, and be what you seem. Speak plainly and truthfully in this era in which words are often used to manipulate rather than illuminate, to hide rather that reveal truth, to make profit rather than good policy, to make us forget rather than learn and listen, to comfort us when we need to be challenged and to change, to help us avoid ourselves and our problems

rather than confront and struggle to solve them. Phonies and calculated performances have become the norm in too much of our political and religious life.[123]

Be a Peacemaker

Resist the urge to bring up motherhood yourself, if you are only able to put it down with sharp-tongued, sarcastic remarks about the dirty work and the thankless hours. Complaining is the easy path—the low road. Choose the high road and you will find that people around you will either be more forthcoming with encouraging remarks and support for motherhood, or they will be so uncomfortable around you that they will leave. Either situation is good. Sometimes it is necessary to make people uncomfortable so that God can begin to work in their hearts.

Do your best to take it all in stride. Don't make life a perpetual crisis. Perpetual crises dull the senses and the body's response mechanisms. Don't cry wolf all the time. Don't let perfection be the enemy of good. Go into a church cathedral or a forest cathedral on occasion and experience the heavenly awe—God's big picture of life. It will give you some perspective on how really trivial, in the grand scheme of motherhood, some of the predicaments are about which we get ourselves worked up into a frenzy—like skipping a nap in order to enjoy the one sunny day of an entire week of rain.

Focus Questions for Making Peace

1. Read 2 Corinthians 5:17–21. How is being a minister of reconciliation for God a step toward peace with motherhood?

2. Is there a specific person who constantly shows disrespect for your mothering choices? How might you "win" this person's respect for your choices based on this chapter and the teaching of 2 Corinthians 5:17–21.

3. Is there a specific occasion when you felt put down because of your home-based, family-centered expectations of motherhood, or that you felt your systems and boundaries were scoffed at or trounced upon? Did you clearly and kindly communicate your perspective and needs beforehand to the person(s) involved? What might you do to stop this from happening again?

Chapter 10

Helping Hands: Where to Look for Help

What does he plant who plants a tree?
He plants a friend of sun and sky;
He plants a flag of breezes free;
The shaft of beauty, towering high;
He plants a home to heaven anigh
For song and mother-croon of bird
in hushed and happy twilight heard—
The treble of heaven's harmony—
These things he plants who plants a tree.
—Henry Cuyler Bunner (1855–1896) (American writer)

In his poem about a tree Bunner is exploring the far-reaching implications, the disseminated impact of a single act—planting a tree. Bearing a child is like this, too.

What does she bear who bears a child?
She bears a friend of kitten and frog;
She bears a haven of stuff stockpiled;
A beam of beauty, in a playpen;
She bears a home to heaven, amen;
For song and sibling-laughter of late
in hushed and giggly twilight await—
The treble of heaven's prologue—
These things she bears who bears a child.
—Heidi Bratton

The widespread impact of bearing a child is staggering. Abraham and Sarah only had one son—Isaac—and yet God promised that through Isaac their descendants would be "as numerous as the stars in the sky and as the sand on the seashore" (Gen 22:17). Sarah laughed at the very idea that she and Abraham could even conceive a son in her old age. And yet today we are her spiritual descendants, a part of the number expanding to fill the heavens.

It is like this for most mothers. We have no concept of the impact that bearing a child will have on ourselves, much less on the world. We give birth having had little or no training for motherhood. We can't overcome the bedtime issues or the food issues with our off-spring, much less attempt family devotions. Going to church on Sunday initiates a grand battle of the wills—little ones and big ones! We have grandiose dreams and desires of being at peace with motherhood, but need some practical help to flesh them out. These helping hands can come from a number of different places. Among them are (1) our parents, (2) the media, (3) friends and mentors, (4) Christian fellowship groups, and (5) professional counselors.

Our Parents

"When I think of who or what was the most helpful in helping me become a good mom," recalls Diane, a mother of four, "my mother comes to mind right away. She was there when each child was born, no matter where we lived. She was the one to give the kids their first bath. She is a nurse, so with each new kid she'd show me how to bathe them, again, and I was thrilled to have her do it even though by the fourth I had it down pretty well. She is very practical and logical, plus she knows each of my kids very well."

"My mother-in-law's dedication to her family was my best example in becoming a mother," says Maria, mother of four. "She was the first woman to show me what it means to stay at home and not resent it. I haven't always taken her advice on how to be my own mother, but I know she doesn't mind. She's given me permission to be me and in doing so, shown me how to let my children be themselves, too." Our own parents, especially our mothers, are obvious choices for us to call on when we need help in becoming mothers ourselves. Our mothers (even our grandmothers, aunts, sisters, and cousins) can be lights to guide our way. They can be fountains of practical wisdom and knowledge about mothering, even if we need to filter some of their advice (as mentioned in Chapter 1), or if they sometimes overflow with more advice than we want to drink in at any one time!

Marian Wright Edelman is an example of a woman whose mother (and father) were beacons of light and fountains of life to her. In her book, *Lanterns: A Memoir of Mentors*, Edelman says, quite simply: "I do what I do because my parents did what they did and were who they were."[124] What Edelman has done on behalf of the civil rights movement that began in the 1960s, and the cause of children in America today, is incredible. As a child and a young adult growing up in a tightly-knit African-American community in Bennettsville, South Carolina, Edelman was surrounded by social and racial unrest. During this era she not only watched her parents minister to the needy and speak the Word of God to a hurting nation, she helped them do it. She went to college, a remarkable achievement for a African-American woman of her day, and became the first and only African-American civil rights lawyer in Mississippi. She later went on to found the *Children's Defense Fund*, which she still runs today. Edelman's legacy of public service and private devotion to the causes of children began with her parents' example of how to genuinely live out the Gospel message of love and service to others. As an adult, Edelman generously gives her parents credit for the practical example they gave her in how to live the same way.

Not every mother enjoys such a close relationship with her parents. Geographical distance from my parents and my in-laws has been an obstacle to the development of close, adult relationships. Both sets of parents, however, have made terrific efforts to span the distance with phone calls, e-mail, and visits when possible; our relationships remain strong despite the distance. One thoughtful way of helping me with motherhood and of keeping our relationship current that my mom has developed is mailing news clippings, books, and even humorous comic strips pertaining to current events of interest to both of us. In fact, at least half the books in my collection on mothering have come from my mom! Occasionally she will highlight portions of an article adding her thoughts to the author's. Sometimes I will send the article back with highlights or comments of my own. In doing this, my mom allows me to digest as much or as little help from the article (and her highlights) as I would like, and to give her feedback whenever time allows.

On one momentous occasion of giving help during our graduate school years, my father accompanied my husband on a two-week quest for fossils in a desolate region of Utah while, at the same time, my mother flew out to Berkeley to help me with the kids in John's absence. To put the magnitude of their help in perspective you need to know that my parents live in Minnesota and work full time. Although my parents were quite young (in their mid-fifties), you can just imagine the change of pace for my father who wears a suit and tie to the office and for my mother who went from caring for zero to four children under the age of six in the span of one plane trip. My parents' helping hands saved the day. Without them we might not have sprung the student-housing trap and escaped from graduate school before the arrival of our fifth child.

The Media as a Helper

Books are wonderful companions that transcend time and place. I have a legion of Christian books, which I look upon as my own personal instructors on the fine art of mothering. The Bible, the book of books, is full of examples from which we can learn what it means to be godly women and mothers: Mary, the mother of Jesus (is there a better example of a mother anywhere?), Ruth (a model of a godly daughter-in-law), Abigail (a wonderful character of courage and action), Mary and Martha (what a team!), Noah's wife (try to image what she went through!). The list goes on. No matter what type of book speaks to your heart, from self-help books to romance novels, from monthly women's magazines to historical biographies, it is possible to surround yourself with literature that is entirely Christ-centered and has been written to make biblical principles relevant for today's culture.

I think, to be honest, that it is from my kids' books and song tapes that I have learned the most about my faith. Truly, our family has had some pretty artistically creative help in applying our Christian faith to our everyday lives. For several years now, the *Adventures in Odyssey* radio drama series, produced by *Focus on the Family*, has been a companion on our entire family's walk with the Lord. We know the characters—Whit, Connie, and Eugene from "Whit's End"—like best friends. My children are of the *Veggie Tale* ® generation for whom characters from the Bible have been freed from the confines of church and have been computer-animated as cartoon vegetables! My experience of the positive influence of Christian media in the building of my children's faith is one of the main motives for using my photography to illustrate Christian children's books (rather than to hang in art galleries). I believe that I can teach children about the love of Jesus—give them their own little legion of helpers—through the photography in my books.

The Internet is the newest communication tool at our disposal. Web sites can provide information for our questions about mothering, and allow us to hear Christian radio programs that are normally aired at times that don't fit into our schedules. Through on-line chatrooms and e-mail it is possible to have a virtual community of friends. E-mail helps me stay in touch with family members, friends, and past mentors, even though we move around quite a bit. The Internet is a powerful tool, but I do have to admit that as the number of my friends that have e-mail has exploded in the last couple of years, I have found it more and more tempting to linger at my computer when my attention should really be on the kids. Somehow that chirpy little "You've got mail" greeting is just so much more inviting than "You've got to sort laundry," "You've got to make dinner," or "I've got homework." I suppose the temptation to escape the house via the Internet is really no different than the temptation to watch TV all day or to retreat into a book. We must be careful not let a good thing be soured by overuse, or become a convenient escape.

Today Bible stories are painted on airwaves and brought to life with plastic figurines, for the same purpose that Michelangelo painted them on the ceiling of the Sistine Chapel and brought them to life from chunks of marble in the 1500s—to dramatize, to teach, and to pass the Christian faith on to the next generation. The greatest part about tapping into various Christian media (don't forget radio talk shows) is that through it, no matter where you live or how frequently you move, you can saturate and surround yourself with practical, godly help in achieving your mothering dreams.

Friends and Mentors

Carrie, a mother of four young children, found other moms to be the most effective helping hands in learning how to be a mother herself. She says: "My own parents have that 'parental amnesia' where they just remember how sweet and good I was at all times. [Someday I will have that same amnesia and I can't wait!] The expert books are good but they can be overwhelming with all of the 'expert advice.' What has helped me is seeing that other families have struggled with the same issues and have made it through. Most of my ideas and the things that have really made a difference for my family have been things I picked up by observing what has worked for other families." A friend can provide you with ideas, examples, and a cup of sugar. A true friend is a sweet blessing on our mothering journeys.

Another place to look for help in fulfilling our mothering aspirations is in mentoring relationships. To be mentored is to be in a friendship with someone whom you trust (usually older) to counsel you in specific areas of your life. A good friend is not the same thing as a mentor. Usually two people agree to enter into a one-on-one mentoring relationship—as an apprentice does with a skilled tradesman—because one needs guidance in an area about which the other is knowledgeable.

Marian Wright Edelman's list of role models is not limited to her parents. Edelman lists many "co-parents"[125] who helped guide her in growing up (elderly women in her church, college professors, etc.). One of the best places to track down some new mentors, or "co-parents," is within the Body of Christ.

Christian Fellowship Groups

The Bible gives women an awesome plan for the art of mother-mentoring. Titus 2:3 admonishes:

Likewise, teach older women to be reverent in the way they live, not to be slanderers or addicted to much wine, but to teach what is good. Then they can train the younger women to love their husbands and children, to be self-controlled and pure, to be busy at home, to be kind, and to be subject to their husbands, so that no one will malign the word of God.

Younger women are to learn from older women, and hopefully, but not exclusively, from their mothers who learned from women older than themselves, who also learned from women older than themselves, and so on back through the generations. It is education distilled to its purest form: teach to others what you learned from others before. Mentor the next generation.

As a new believer in Christ during college, I had the opportunity to receive mentoring from Mary, a volunteer InterVarsity staff worker who "adopted" me and provided for me, through weekly Bible study and heated discussions of relevant social issues, an entirely Christ-centered world view that I had not previously experienced. Her mentoring made a difference in my life. Her mentoring helped me become a new creation in Christ. Her mentoring impacted my marriage, is impacting how I am raising my children, and will impact how my children choose their friends and mates and raise their own children. As a tree grows and expands to fill the sky, so is Mary's mentoring influence expanding to fill heaven.

As a grown woman and mother, it has been my experience that joining or beginning a Bible study at our local church has been a good way to meet new friends and potential mentors. Where this was not possible, I joined a parachurch Bible study like *Community Bible Study (CBS)*, or a fellowship group like MOPS. In these Christian-based groups, which largely follow the biblical model presented in Titus 2:3, you will find moms with whom you can share common interests and priorities. Some churches have an official ministry of "spiritual direction" to help members connect in mentoring relationships. Some churches have women's fellowship groups or action committees that facilitate less formal mentoring relationships between church members. If you are estranged from your family (even if only geographically), or if you move frequently, joining any one of these groups can help you to get plugged into new friendships fairly quickly, or begin finding mentors.

Beyond the Need for Mentoring

Elisa Morgan is a mom who needed more help than could be provided by a mentor or a few good books. Raised by a divorced, alcoholic mother, Morgan herself admits that she is "probably the least likely person to head a mothering organization," yet God called her to be the president of MOPS. In her monthly column in *Christian Parenting Today*, Morgan shared:

> While my mother meant well—truly she did—most of my memories are of me mothering her rather than her mothering me. Alcohol altered her love, turning it into something that wasn't love....A mother's love may sometimes fail, but God's love takes even the imperfect love of an imperfect mother and uses it to shape his perfect design in the life of her child.[126]

Elisa Morgan sought after God's will in her life. She prayed for God's call in her life and found it to be helping moms whose needs mirrored her own. Morgan also sought professional therapy and understands better now, as a mother of two adopted children herself, why her mother felt she needed the crutch of alcohol.[127]

If you are struggling beyond your ability to cope, you may need to seek out some professional help. Modern psychology offers many helpful insights into recovering from learned dysfunctional behaviors (such as codependency) that we may have acquired during our childhoods or at any time in our lives. Counselors can help us identify chemical disorders that we never asked for (like clinical depression) but find we need to address. As adults, we need to realize that we are fully responsible for our own actions. When addressing the need for serious behavior modification, professional helping hands can be invaluable in assisting us in changing for the better.

The generational, manifold impact of bearing a child is as far-reaching as planting a tree. The impact that our mothering will have on our children and future generations is as unfathomable as the aggregate grains of sand on the seashore or the multitudinous stars in the sky. Because we want our impact to be one of peace and blessing, we need to reach out for help in areas of need or weakness. It is entirely possible that the choice you make to seek peace with motherhood, to rearrange or postpone your personal goals and ambitions so that you can be a blessing to your children, will be a blessing of peace that goes forth until God's Kingdom comes here on Earth.

Don't laugh, like Sarah did. Instead hang onto the helping hands and believe, like the Virgin Mary did, that your making peace with motherhood will be an ever-expanding blessing to your children, and to their children. "No eye has seen, no ear has heard, no mind has conceived what God has prepared for those who love him" (1 Cor 2:9, quoting Isa 64:4). Or as the angel said to Jesus' mother, "For nothing is impossible with God" (Luke 1:3).

Focus Questions for Making Peace

1. Read Proverbs 22:6 and Deuteronomy 6:6–7. According to these verses, when and how should you train up your children in the faith? What promise is given for the child trained up this way?

2. From what helping hands have you benefited most in motherhood in learning how to train up your children?

3. Read Titus 2:3–5. Are you in an ongoing Christian mentoring relationship? If you are a more mature Christian, is there someone younger in the faith that you could take under your wing? If you are younger, is there someone from whom you could seek godly counsel? If yes, please do it! If you are unsure, begin to pray for God to bring such a person into your life.

Chapter 11

Faithful Not Fearful Mothers: Letting God In on Mothering

"Mommy, will you keep track of my footprints?" three-year-old Lucy asked. I laughed and asked her what she meant. "You know, Mommy! Like you did with the big kids and the crabs," she patiently explained to her confused mother. When she mentioned the crabs, I understood. We had been the first ones to arrive at the beach that bright summer morning. It was a beautiful white sandy beach near our home on Cape Cod that had a marvelous salt marsh just behind the main beach. The tide was fairly low and still going out, so I had been pointing out to the kids all of the animal tracks and ripples left on the sand.

We found footprints left by seagulls and sandpipers. We were able to locate clams by digging out the small holes that they made in the sand with their siphons. We detected the presence of fiddler crabs by observing larger holes in the sandy banks of the salt marsh. (None of us was brave enough to stick a finger in one of the holes to see if there were actually crabs in there!) We collected feathers and speculated about which birds had lost them there. We traced the lowering of the tide by the wave patterns left on the sand as the water receded down the sand bar.

Having pursued all these tracks, evidence of things living at the beach that we never actually saw, Lucy wanted someone to pursue her, to keep watch for her, and to keep track of her, too. She wanted to know, in her three-year-old way, that she was important—that she was a significant part of the group assembled, significant enough to be looked for after she was gone. Being careful not to cover up her footprints with my own, I raced all over the beach following my giggling Lucy, keeping track of her footprints. It was a divine mothering morning.

How natural it is for each of us to want to be significant—to know that our contributions to family, to our place of work or volunteering, to our children's educations, to our churches, and to our world are worthy of someone's keeping track. We want to know that we, as mothers, have left our mark, our imprint on our children, even after we are gone. Egotistical? I don't think so. It is a desire as natural as Lucy's wanting her mother, the most important person in her young world, to keep track of her footprints.

In order for us to make a lasting contribution to the world through motherhood and throughout the many different seasons of motherhood, we must address one last thing: FEAR. Fear of ruining our children forever if we use a pacifier. Fear of not being able to pay the bills this month, much less save for college. Fear of failing. In the face of fear we must listen to faith. The fear we must combat with faith is twofold: first is fear which manifests itself as doubt of our ability to deal with the difficulties of current known situations; second is fear of the unknown future.

Fear of Today

The first kind of fear, our doubt of being able to deal with known situations, is the kind that asks: But what if I married the wrong guy? Our marriage seems impossible. But what if God wanted me to have more children? Or fewer? What if I was supposed to have taken *that* job? Or moved to *that* city? What if I had enrolled my child in *that* school? What if? What if? Doubt about the present robs us of peace in the now and paralyzes us from making good choices for the future.

We cannot begin to make peace with motherhood, to move toward being home-based and family-centered, toward making life-giving choices for our families and ourselves, until we have made peace with our doubts about the present. And truly our doubts are a lack of faith. Fear reveals our doubt in God's sovereignty in our lives.

Forget the specifics of your situation for a minute and ask yourself if your God is so small that he can't make good come out of your mistakes. Even Christians sin and make mistakes. Don't you believe that God can forgive them? That he can heal your wounds? That he can take your honest questions and deep searching? Can you believe that God is really, *really*, REALLY big? Have faith. God really is really big.

Fear of the Future

The second kind of fear, the fear of the unknown future, is twinned with the fear of failure. This is the kind of fear that enslaves one to a known situation, even if it is a bad situation, because it is too scary to risk a new, unknown situation, even if it could be better. Maria Shriver's book, *Ten Things I Wish I'd Known—Before I Went Out into the Real World,* was based on a speech she gave at a college graduation. Shriver summed up her advice to the graduates with this thought:

> I know you're wondering whether that jittery feeling in your gut is excitement or just plain fear of the future. Believe me, it's fear. Fear of the unknown and the fear of failure—in love and in life. It's all right and perfectly normal and natural to be anxious about what's around the corner. But never let that stop you from looking around the corner to see what's there for you.[128]

Lesson 5 in Edelman's book, *The Measure of Our Success,* is:

> Don't be afraid of taking risks or of being criticized. An anonymous sage said, "If you don't want to be criticized don't say anything, don't

do anything, or be anything." Don't be afraid of failing. It's the way you learn to do things right. It doesn't matter how many times you fall down. What matters is how many times you get up.[129]

In other words, falling down is a part of the journey, a part that I experienced recently. My third baby, Olivia, was headed to kindergarten, and as September approached I began mourning the loss of not having her at home. For the first time in eight years I was not expecting a new baby to replace the one catching the school bus. It was time for a premature crisis of the type I talked about in Chapter 2 (the Off-to-Kindergarten identity crisis). With baby #3 at school, I would *only* have two munchkins at home in the morning (Lucy, 3 1/2, and Benjamin, almost 2). Relative to the recent summer months of having all five home all day, it seemed like a breeze.

During July and August of that same summer, several exciting photography and book projects were coming together that I knew would require more time from me to be successfully brought to market. But I was afraid. Olivia's going to kindergarten would free up the necessary time that I needed, but the freedom was replaced by the fear that because of my new-found time I would *have* to succeed with these projects.

But what if I didn't succeed? What if I both lost my child to kindergarten and failed to bring my new books into being? In the midst of this fear I awoke one morning with an overwhelmingly powerful desire to have a sixth child. For me, because of severe circulation problems due to varicose veins caused by pregnancy, this was a completely irrational desire. I knew having a sixth child would be very risky for both the baby and me. So intense was my desire, however, that I called my husband at work and told him what I was feeling just to get it off my chest—to hear him laugh and call me crazy. Well, he did laugh, and said he'd be happy to help me out when he got home after work, *if* another baby was what I really wanted.

Fortunately, by that evening I had regained perspective and realized that it was fear of the unknown, the impending change in mothering seasons, that was causing me to feel so irrational. I was stumbling over fear.

My yearning for a new baby was not about wanting a "baby"—a new little life to nurture. It was about having a scapegoat, a convenient reason why I couldn't even attempt the new challenges I faced, and therefore not have to risk failure. I was afraid of facing a season of mothering I had never known—one without an infant nestled to my breast while I juggled everything and everyone else. I was afraid of the increased expectations of having such comparative mobility.

I was asking to return to the known "slavery" of bed rest and infant-care, like the Israelite nation pleading to return to slavery in Egypt out of fear of not knowing how God would provide for their impending trek across an unknown desert in search of the Promised Land. Just like them, I was afraid because I did not know how God was going to guide me and provide for me as I wandered my way into the next season of motherhood.

Stephanie, a mother expecting her fifth child, shares an experience of wanting to move on to the next season of motherhood, and yet being unsure—fearful of jumping ahead of God's plan.

I always wanted a large family and since I already had two girls and two boys I felt that was the perfect number. I could handle this many and I was ready to expand my horizons, to become something more "significant." I felt that I'd been selfless long enough and that now it was time for me to search for those hidden talents or perhaps to use my back-burner gifts. Yet, something inside was pulling at my soul. Then, one day my husband asked me to attend Marriage Encounter. I reluctantly went and all I talked about on the drive there was all the reasons I had decided that I was done having children. I remained open to the good Lord blessing me again, but I was not choosing it.

Well, something changed on that weekend. Inspired by prayer and the extraordinary example of the faith of Joseph, Jesus' earthly father (a simple man through whom, by his acceptance of God's will, many great things happened), I realized that I felt simple, useless, unable to do much and that motherhood, at times, seemed to hinder me in doing great things for God. And yet I realized something more. My simple "yes" has brought four beautiful children into the world. Just like Joseph's, my "yes" to life is noble, honorable, and a worthy calling. My time spent in motherhood may be simple in the public eye, but it is more profound. These children are the future and they could make a difference in the world. How I raise them will affect that outcome. So I said yes, again, to the Lord, because a child is an investment in the Kingdom of God.

Jennifer experienced yet another type of fear of the unknown future that pierces the heart of a woman who desires to be a good mother: infertility.

My best lesson in motherhood was learned through our three years of miscarriages and infertility; that is, that children are truly a blessing, not something to be taken for granted. Having the memory of the fear that we would never be parents etched in my mind will help me truly appreciate every trial and tribulation we encounter with our children. I am enjoying and appreciating every step of the way with our [one-year-old] daughter and my current pregnancy. We don't sweat the small stuff anymore. Our priorities are clearly defined.

My Prayers for the Future of Motherhood

My prayer for the future of motherhood, yours and mine, as I have shared in this book, is that your priorities would be clearly defined and that you would be encouraged and strengthened to act on them. Some of the ideas and ideals of motherhood that I've written about are but dreams to the majority of women who are mothering children right now. But we must not be afraid to help them make peace with motherhood, too. Long-term victory takes place one day at a time. Neither you nor I have to muster up the enthusiasm or the energy to change our children or our church—to push for better programs or more involvement from other parents. That's what faith is for.

What we need to do is pray and to keep standing up for the mothering we believe in. Consider Psalm 1:2–3 (I change *he* to *she* here for feminine emphasis): "But her delight is in the law of the LORD, and on his law she meditates day and night. She is like a tree planted by streams of water which yields its fruit in season and whose leaf does not wither. Whatever she does prospers." Also consider Psalm 12:7: "Because of the oppression of the weak and the groaning of the needy, I will now arise," says the LORD, "I will protect them from those who malign them." God will do the changing for us. I haven't written about making peace with motherhood just to increase your knowledge and understanding, but to transform your motherhood into a life full of joy and zeal. I want you to live victoriously in every circumstance because of God's grace and his providence. I want you to have an internal peace about motherhood that cannot be affected by external situations. I want you to have peace— a deep-seated peace that penetrates to your very heart—because if you have a child, then motherhood is an integral part of living up to your full potential as a woman. It is not a thing apart from who you are or a nice addition to your cozy, compartmentalized life. Motherhood is a part of the living, dynamic essence of who God made you to be.

For the benefit of the next generation, that of my daughters and potential daughters-in-law, I would like to see the hopes I have mentioned in this book become reality. Here are my highest hopes, my primary prayers for motherhood:

(1) I pray that you—a mother of today—will make peace with motherhood. Take action on your heart's desire for peace. I pray that you will be able to separate yourself from the unrealistic and false

expectations with which you are saddled by the popular media, your peers, and the generation before you. I pray that you will grasp what a gift motherhood is.

(2) I pray that you can untie your identity and self-worth from your relationships, responsibilities, and possessions. I pray that Super-Mom will go back to her own planet. I pray that you can forgive yourself for the things that have not worked out and move on. I pray that you can let go of your unrealistic expectation of having and doing everything in life all at once. Please pray the same for me.

(3) I pray that we can reclaim the value of homemaking. Let's begin to view home not as the over-decorated jail of a bored, bon-bon-eating housewife, but as the domain of a purpose-filled, family-centered professional entrusted with the responsibility of creating a loving and peaceful environment in which to responsibly raise the next generation. It's a daunting job.

Mothers who have always worked outside the home full time, I hope that you have been encouraged to see your job as a mother in a new, more impressive light as you read this book. Perhaps you are still tempted to remain work-centered, not because of any great love of your job, but because of the familiar slavery of juggling work, home, and childcare. Perhaps you are afraid of the unfamiliar freedom of not reporting to a boss or of depending on your husband financially. Do not be afraid. Have the courage. Believe in God's call for you in this new season of motherhood, whether it involves working outside your home or not. Be brave enough to believe that he can part the sea of conflicts that stands in the way of your becoming home-based and family-centered.

Mothers who have always put their children's interests first, to the detriment of their own well-being, do not be afraid. It is okay to have interests of your own. I pray that you will take off your hair shirt and give up the martyr's identity. Insecurity is in fact a severe type of slavery. Brave the world outside of your home. Have the courage to believe that your gifts and talents are useful and that they can be a pleasing complement to your family life. I pray that you will pursue your passions in God's season.

(4) I pray for a continued increase in our cultural esteem of home-based activities for women with children, such as volunteer work, home-schooling, home-based businesses, and flexible employment opportunities outside the home.

(5) I pray that women (and men) will begin to laugh, out loud, at the corrupt worldview that says motherhood is a waste of a college education. If beauty is a reward in and of itself, so is education, especially when it is applied toward raising the next generation.

(6) I ask that you will pray for and work toward healing within the Body of Christ. I will be praying for it, too.

(7) I pray that you will let God in on your spiritual and physical balancing acts. Remember, the key to balance is priorities. Love God first. Celebrate your situation second. Live life in its season third. In every situation remember to balance your use of time, space, and money. To every season remember to apply initiative, contentment, and faithfulness.

(8) At the bureaucratic, public-funding level, I pray for economic support for active, engaged parenting by the shifting of government funds from child-care alternatives to parent-care initiatives—from subsidized daycare centers to extended family-leave policies and family-support services. At the corporate level I pray for a rapid multiplication of "mommy tracks." Home offices, e-commerce, job sequencing, and job sharing—these are all economically smart and kid-friendly business strategies. Let's push for them.

I hope and pray that we as a nation can begin to evaluate a mother's worth not on a cash basis, but on the contributions mothers make to the security, confidence, and education of our children—the next generation of leaders. It is important for us to change the cultural tide—the economic perspective that mothering *is not* a worthwhile use of a woman's time and energy—to the sure knowledge that mothering *is* the best investment we can make in the future of our country. We need to reclaim the word *mother*. Never again disfigure the word *mother* with "just-a—." Never.

(9) I pray that mothers would mentor their daughters, remaining actively involved in helping their daughters and granddaughters to become mothers in their own right.

For women who are either physically, emotionally, or spiritually separated from their own mothers or their own daughters, I pray for the development of serious and ongoing mentoring relationships with other women and church communities that foster these relationships.

(10) I pray that we can all begin to live life in its season—striving not for the finish line, but for harvest time. I pray that you can see your children as seedlings—newborn gifts from God. I pray that you can see and act on the importance of caring for your family—your garden—personally.

Have No Fear

While writing this book I have been infinitely mindful and afraid of a self-critique written by Anne Morrow Lindbergh of her book, *Gift from the Sea*, twenty years after its original publication in 1955. An eloquent writer and deeply insightful mother of five children, Lindbergh confesses that she very much underestimated the difficulties of the forthcoming years, since she was still deluged in the child-rearing years while she was writing her book:

Next comes an embarrassed astonishment at re-reading my naïve assumption in the book that the "victories" in women's coming of age had been largely won by the Feminists of my mother's generation. I realize in hindsight and humility how great and how many were—and are—the victories still to be won.[130]

Peace is one of those victories to be won. Peace with ourselves. Peace with motherhood. Peace with how we bring the two together. I'm sure that some of the prayers I've outlined in this book are as naïve as Lindbergh's assumptions because I write, as she did, while still very much in the midst of active mothering duty. And yet, despite the risk of espousing a sophomoric grasp of peace, I write for the opportunity to reach those mothers of my generation who are not at peace with motherhood—those mothers who are shaping the spouses with whom, and the cultural environment in which, my children might someday parent their own children.

Because I believe it is possible that together we can make peace with motherhood and thereby restore honor to the job of mothering, and bring the feminist movement to true fruition, I have not been shy in sharing my prayers, hopes, and dreams with you. Don't be afraid, either, to share yours with other mothers.

I agree with what Marian Wright Edelman says about the potential of our impact on the future:

> I do not seek to reinvent the past or think we can stop the bulldozer of "progress" ushered in by technology and by the globalization of our economy. I do think, though, that we must stop and assess what we have gained and what we have lost over the past half century, and how we might adjust our institutions to meet changing child and family needs in a positive rather than in a punitive or impersonal way.[131]

Not back to the good old days, but to a new time where there is peace in our own hearts and where unity exists among women where the good of our children is concerned.

As our bodies have been changed to carry the gift of life, so can our hearts be changed to embrace peace in God's call to be a mother. Motherhood is a combination of pleasure and exhaustion, especially in the early years. It is endless, all-consuming, boring, and repetitive as often as it is delightful, fulfilling, lovely, and exuberant, but motherhood is not a labor camp. Oh, yes, it involves sacrifice and postponing many of our own needs and goals, but motherhood is not punishment. It is a privilege! It is a privilege to carry life in our womb and to nurture that life through childhood. I encourage you—I challenge you—to make peace with that privilege.

Focus Questions for Making Peace

1. Read 2 Timothy ·1:7. List anything that you are afraid of in your current mothering life. How can knowing that God did not give us a spirit of timidity (or fear) but of power (or confident ability), of love, and of self-discipline, help you overcome that fear?

2. Read Philippians 4:13. What can you do through Christ?

3. Go back to your list from question 1 and put a check mark next to the ones of which you are most afraid. Begin to pray, through Christ, for the ability to conquer these fears in the future. Share those fears (that you are comfortable sharing) with your friends and/or mentors who will pray with and for you.

Epilogue: Sing Your Own Song

Recently we went to a performance of *Riverdance* in Boston. Unrivaled in its exposition of Irish dancing and music, the performance was incredible. One performer, a female violinist, caught my attention. Unlike any violinist I have ever seen before, her manner was not serious, and she was not staring trance-like at her violin. She was vivacious! She looked up and out at her audience—at me—and invited us to dance! At one point in the program she literally jumped off the back stage and paraded around the main stage, breaking strands of her bow as she sawed with strong, vibrant strokes of musical energy. She embodied her music. She embodied passion. She was pure zest.

Her performance rekindled in me the urge to fling myself into womanhood—into motherhood. She brought to new birth my desire to be passionate about all that I hold dear because life is good! In communion with her performance, I could understand the fervor of heaven—singing alleluia with all the angels and saints before the very throne of God. I was filled with a fiery desire for the fullness of life. At long last, I knew in my heart that I had made peace with motherhood.

I went away from that evening encouraged by my fellow artist to be a part of the music and to pursue with passion my mothering, my photography, my *everything*. I was ready to sing a new song. Ready to embrace the mundane and to gracefully dance with the practical.

Ready to joyously give thanks for the opportunity to be a woman and to have the privilege of being a mother.

Now is the time for you to sing your own song, mom. Without fear lavish yourself, your time, energy, and money—your heart and soul—on your call to motherhood. Don't wait until the kids are in school, or the car is paid off, or anything else before you answer God's special call in your life. Sing your own song—each note and each rest in its time, each song in its season. Our world, your children's world, will be a better place because you did.

Notes

1. Alexandra Stoddard, *Mothers: A Celebration* (New York: William Morrow & Co., 1996), p. 48.

2. Susan Mushart, *The Mask of Motherhood* (New York: New York Press, 1999), p. xviii.

3. Jill Smolowe, et al., "Mom on a Mission," *People* magazine, June 19, 2000, p. 128.

4. Maria Shriver, *Ten Things I Wish I'd Known—Before I Went Out into the Real World* (New York: Warner Books, 2000), pp. 77–79.

5. Laura Schlessinger, *Parenthood by Proxy* (New York: HarperCollins Publishers, 2000), p. 3.

6. Anne Roiphe, *Fruitful* (New York: Houghton Mifflin Co., 1996), p. 11.

7. *American Photography, A Century of Images*, Public Broadcasting Service (PBS), produced by KTCA, St. Paul/Minneapolis, 1999.

8. Ibid.

9. Danielle Crittenden, *What Our Mothers Didn't Tell Us, Focus on the Family* radio interview, aired March 2000.

10. Danielle Crittenden, *What Our Mothers Didn't Tell Us* (New York: Simon and Schuster, 1999), p. 17.

11. Schlessinger, *Parenthood by Proxy*, p. 2.

12. Crittenden, *What Our Mothers Didn't Tell Us*, pp. 20–21.

13. Roiphe, *Fruitful*, p. 233.

14. Shriver, *Ten Things I Wish I'd Known*, p. 73.

15. Michael Collopy, *Works of Love are Works of Peace* (San Francisco: Ignatius Press, 1996), p. 105.

16. Crittenden, *What Our Mothers Didn't Tell Us*, p. 121.

17. Shriver, *Ten Things I Wish I'd Known*, p. 62.

18. Collopy, *Works of Love are Works of Peace*, p. 35.

19. Maushart, *The Mask of Motherhood*, pp. 1–4.

20. Philip Yancey, *What's So Amazing About Grace?* (Grand Rapids, Mich.: Zondervan Publishing House, 1997), p. 202.

21. Connie Fourre Zimney, *In Praise of Homemaking* (Notre Dame, Ind.: Ave Maria Press, 1984), p. 19.

22. Ibid., p. 22.

23. Betty Friedan, *The Feminine Mystique* (New York: Dell Publishing, 1963), p. 14.

24. From an interview with the author.

25. Susan Schaeffer Macaulay, *For The Children's Sake* (Wheaton, Ill.: Good News Publishers, 1984), p. 47.

26. Larry Burkett, *Women Leaving the Workplace* (Chicago: Moody Press, 1995), pp. 99–100.

27. Jane Sellman, as quoted in an e-mail forward titled "Fun Quotes from Women."

28. Jill Savage, *Professionalizing Motherhood* (Grand Rapids, Mich.: Zondervan Publishing House, 2001), back cover.

29. Ibid., p. 25.

30. Maushart, *The Mask of Motherhood*, p. xx.

31. Paula Peters, "Back on Track," *Cape Cod Times*, Section B, March 12, 2000, p. 1.

32. Angie Peters, *Celebrate Home* (St. Louis: Concordia Publishing House, 1998), p. 164.

33. Ibid.

34. Brenda Hunter, *Home by Choice* (Sisters, Ore.: Questar Publishing, 1991), p. 49.

35. T. Berry Brazelton, and Stanley Greenspan, "Our Window to the Future," Fall/Winter 2000 Special Edition of Newsweek's *Your Child* magazine, p. 34.

36. Ibid., p. 36.

37. Thomas Hayden, "A Sense of Self," Fall/Winter 2000 Special Edition of Newsweek's *Your Child* magazine, p. 58.

38. Stephen Covey, *The 7 Habits of Highly Effective People* (New York: Simon and Schuster, 1989), p. 97.

39. Ibid., p. 98.

40. Shriver, *Ten Things I Wish I'd Known*, pp. 1 and 8.

41. Cynthia Tobias, *The Way They Learn* (Colorado Springs, Colo.: Focus on the Family Publishing, 1994), Chapter 2.

42. Helen Boursier, *Tell It with Style* (Downers Grove, Ill.: InterVarsity Press, 1995), pp. 14–15.

43. Ibid., p. 16.

44. Ibid., p. 17.

45. Tobias, *The Way They Learn*, p. 17.

46. Dr. Mary Ann Froehlich, *What's a Smart Woman Like You Doing in a Place Like This?* (Brentwood, Tenn.: Wolgemuth and Hyatt Publishers, 1989), back cover.

47. Ibid., p. 24.

48. Ibid., back cover.

49. Macaulay, *For the Children's Sake*, p. 90.

50. "World Vision's 10 Urgent Issues List," *World Vision Today*, Spring 2000, p. 3. www.wvi.org.

51. Ibid., p. 12.

52. Burkett, *Women Leaving the Workplace*, p. 146.

53. Gladys Hunt, *Honey for a Child's Heart* (Grand Rapids, Mich.: Zondervan Publishing House, 1989), p. 113.

54. Brian D. Ray, Fact Sheet IIe, National Home Education Research Institute, Salem, Oreg., www.nhevi.org.

55. Dana Mack, *Assault on Parenthood* (New York: Simon and Schuster, 1997), p. 236.

56. Ibid.

57. Collopy, *Works of Love Are Works of Peace*, p. 35.

58. Mother Teresa of Calcutta, 1979 Nobel Peace Prize acceptance speech.

59. Charles Colson, with Ellen Vaughn, *The Body* (Dallas: Word Publishing, 1996), p. 85.

60. Ibid., p. 84.

61. Thomas P. Rausch, *Catholics and Evangelicals: Do They Share a Common Future?* (Mahwah, N.J.: Paulist Press, 2000), pp. 47–48.

62. Ibid.

63. James Dunbar, "Catholic, Lutheran Clergy Mark Pact," *The Anchor*, Nov. 5, 1999, p. 1.

64. Colson, *The Body*, p. 82.

65. Ibid., p. 84.

66. Diane Bock, as quoted in: Betty Cortina, "She Found the Courage to Fight Racism," O magazine, July/Aug. 2000, p. 53.

67. Yancey, *What's So Amazing About Grace?* pp. 130–133, 193–210.

68. Rausch, *Catholics and Evangelicals: Do They Share a Common Future?* p. 51.

69. Ibid.

70. Yancey, *What's So Amazing About Grace?* p. 210.

71. Ada Lum, *Luke: New Hope, New Joy*, Lifeguide Bible Studies (Downers Grove, Ill.: InterVarsity Press, 1992), p. 33.

72. Susan Alexander Yates, *And Then I Had Kids* (Grand Rapids, Mich.: Baker Books, 2001), p. 25.

73. Maushart, *The Mask of Motherhood*, p. xx.

74. Rob Parsons, "Almost Everything I Need to Know about God I Learned in Sunday School," *Focus on the Family* Magazine, February, 2000, p. 7.

75. Elizabeth Hoffman Reed, *Gathering at the Table* (Chicago: Liturgy Training Press, 1999), p. 7.

76. James Gleick, "Faster: The Acceleration of Just about Everything," book excerpt from *Reader's Digest*, March, 2000, p. 66.

77. "In Defense of Boredom," *Offspring* magazine, June/July, 2000, p. 96.

78. Ibid.

79. Mary Manz Simon, "Ask Dr. Mary" advice column, *Christian Parenting Today*, March/April 2000, p. 11.

80. Hunt, *Honey for a Child's Heart*, pp. 116–117.

81. Ibid., p. 110.

82. Quoted by Laurie Ashcraft in: Patricia Edmonds, "What Women Want Now," *USA Weekend* magazine, *Minneapolis Star Tribune*, October 23–25, 1998, p. 5.

83. James Dobson, *Life on The Edge: Young Adults' Guide to a Meaningful Future* (Dallas: Word Publishing, 1995), p. 281.

84. Mary Manz Simon, "Surrounded by Stuff," *Christian Parenting Today*, May/June 1999, p. 50.

85. John Michael Talbot, with Dan O'Neill, *Simplicity* (Ann Arbor, Mich.: Servant Publications, 1989), p. xiv–xv.

86. Paul L. Wachtel, *The Poverty of Affluence* (Philadelphia: New Society Publishers, 1989), back cover.

87. Amy Dacyczyn, *The Tightwad Gazette* (New York: Villard Books, 1993), front cover.

88. Crittenden, *What Our Mothers Didn't Tell Us*, p. 122.

89. Ibid., pp. 133–134.

90. Schlessinger, *Parenthood by Proxy*, pp. 77–78.

91. Arlie Russell Hochschild, *The Time Bind* (New York: Henry Holt and Company, 1997), Chapters 13–14.

92. Hunter, *Home by Choice*, p. 84.

93. Ibid.

94. Connie Marshner, *Can Motherhood Survive?* (Brentwood, Tenn.: Wolgemuth and Hyatt, Publishers, 1990), p. 204.

95. Crittenden, *What Our Mothers Didn't Tell Us*, p. 133.

96. Burkett, *Women Leaving the Workplace*, p. 14.

97. Genesis 2:18–25.

98. Yates, *And Then I Had Kids*, p. 75.

99. James Dobson, "Family News from Dr. James Dobson," in *Focus on the Family magazine*, June 2000, p. 2.

100. Shriver, *Ten Things I Wish I'd Known*, p. 89.

101. Marian Wright Edelman, *Lanterns: A Memoir of Mentors* (Boston: Beacon Press, 1999), p. 161.

102. E-mail forward copied from a 1960 high school Home Economics workbook.

103. Crittenden, *What Our Mothers Didn't Tell Us*, p. 84.

104. Hunter, *Home by Choice*, p. 170.

105. Crittenden, *What Our Mothers Didn't Tell Us*, p. 84.

106. Becky Tirabassi, *Being a Wild, Wacky, Wonderful Woman for God* (Grand Rapids, Mich.: Zondervan Publishing House, 1994), p. 62.

107. Mack, *Assault on Parenthood*, p. 282.

108. Pat Holt and Grace Ketterman, *When You Feel Like Screaming* (Wheaton, Illinois: Harold Shaw Publishers, 1988), pp. 57–58.

109. Mack, *Assault on Parenthood*, p. 179.

110. Marian Wright Edelman, *The Measure of Our Success* (Boston: Beacon Press, 1992), pp. 43–44.

111. Ibid., p. 80, quoting National Conference of Catholic Bishops' pastoral letter, "Putting Children and Families First: A Challenge for our Church, Nation, and World," November, 1991, p. 7.

112. Ibid., p. 80.

113. Mack, *Assault on Parenthood*, p. 282.

114. Ibid., p. 292.

115. Ronald S. Wilson, "Before Affirmative Action," *Brown Alumni Monthly*, March/April, 2000, pp. 47–48.

116. Mack, *Assault on Parenthood*, p. 293.

117. Edelman, *Lanterns*, p. 157.

118. Mack, *Assault on Parenthood*, p. 293.

119. Ibid., pp. 292–293.

120. Eugene Lee-Hamilton, as quoted by Michelle Lovric, *The Forests* (Philadelphia: Running Press Book Publishers, 1996), p. 26.

121. Gwen Weisling, *Raising Kids on Purpose for the Fun of It* (Old Tappan, New Jersey: Fleming H. Revell Company, 1989), p. 84.

122. Gwen Weisling Ellis, *Thriving as a Working Woman* (Wheaton, Illinois: Tyndale House Publishers, 1995), p. 189.

123. Edelman, *Lanterns*, p. 164.

124. Ibid., p. 3.

125. Ibid., p. 10.

126. Elisa Morgan, "The Upside of an Upside-Down Life," *Christian Parenting Today*, May/June, 1999, p. 64.

127. Ibid.

128. Shriver, *Ten Things I Wish I'd Known*, p. 117.

129. Edelman, *The Measure of Our Success*, p. 42.

130. Anne Morrow Lindbergh, *Gift From the Sea* (New York: Random House, 1997), pp. 131–132.

131. Edelman, *Lanterns: A Memoir of Mentors*, p. 17.

Bibliography

American Photography: A Century of Images. Public Broadcasting Service, 1999.

Boursier, Helen T. *Tell It With Style.* Downers Grove, Illinois: InterVarsity Press, 1995.

Brazelton, T. Berry, and Stanley Greenspan. "Our Window to the Future." Special Edition of Newsweek's *Your Child* magazine, Fall/Winter 2000.

Burkett, Larry. *Women Leaving the Workplace.* Chicago: Moody Press, 1995.

Collopy, Michael. *Works of Love Are Works of Peace.* San Francisco: Ignatius Press, 1996.

Colson, Charles, with Ellen Vaughn. *The Body.* Dallas: Word Publishing, 1996.

Cortina, Betty. "She Found the Courage to Fight Racism." O magazine, July/August 2000.

Covey, Stephen R. *The 7 Habits of Highly Effective People.* New York: Simon and Schuster, 1989.

Crittenden, Danielle. *What Our Mothers Didn't Tell Us.* New York: Simon and Schuster, 1999.

Crittenden, Danielle. *What Our Mothers Didn't Tell Us. Focus on the Family* radio interview, aired March 2000, Part I, tape number CT265/24419.

Dacyczyn, Amy. *The Tightwad Gazette.* New York: Villard Books, 1993.

Dobson, James. *Life on The Edge: Young Adults' Guide to a Meaningful Future.* Dallas: Word Publishing, 1995.

Dunbar, James. "Catholic, Lutheran Clergy Mark Pact." *The Anchor* newspaper, Diocese of Fall River Mass., November 5, 1999.

Edelman, Marian Wright. *The Measure of Our Success*. Boston: Beacon Press, 1992.

Edelman, Marian Wright. *Lanterns: A Memoir of Mentors*. Boston: Beacon Press, 1999.

Edmonds, Patricia. "What Women Want Now." *USA Weekend* magazine, *Minneapolis Star Tribune*, October 23–25, 1998.

Ellis, Gwen. *Thriving as a Working Woman*. Wheaton, Illinois: Tyndale House Publishers, 1995.

Friedan, Betty. *The Feminine Mystique*. New York: Dell Publishing Company, 1963.

Froehlich, Mary Ann. *What's a Smart Woman Like You Doing In a Place Like This?* Brentwood, Tennessee: Wolgemuth & Hyatt Publishers, 1989.

Gleick, James. "Faster: The Acceleration of Just About Everything" (book excerpt). *Reader's Digest*, March, 2000, p. 96.

Hayden, Thomas. "A Sense of Self." *Your Child*, special edition of *Newsweek* magazine, Fall/Winter 2000.

Hochschild, Arlie Russell. *Time Bind*. New York: Henry Holt and Company, 1997.

Holt, Pat, and Grace Ketterman. *When You Feel Like Screaming*. Wheaton, Illinois: Harold Shaw Publishers, 1988.

Hunt, Gladys. *Honey for a Child's Heart*. Grand Rapids, Michigan: Zondervan Publishing House, 1989.

Hunter, Brenda. *Home by Choice*. Sisters, Oreg.: Questar Publishing, 1991.

"In Defense of Boredom." *Offspring* magazine, June/July 2000.

Lindbergh, Anne Morrow. *Gift From the Sea*. New York: Random House, 1997.

Lovric, Michelle. *The Forests*. Philadelphia: Running Press Book Publishers, 1996.

Lum, Ada. *Luke: New Hope, New Joy*. Lifeguide Bible Studies. Downers Grove, Illinois: InterVarsity Press, 1992.

Bibliography

Macaulay, Susan Schaeffer. *For the Children's Sake*. Wheaton, Illinois: Good News Publishers, 1984.

Mack, Dana. *Assault on Parenthood*. New York: Simon and Schuster, 1997.

Marshner, Connie. *Can Motherhood Survive?* Brentwood, Tennessee: Wolgemuth & Hyatt Publishers, 1990.

Maushart, Susan. *The Mask of Motherhood*. New York: New York Press, 1999.

Morgan, Elisa. "The Upside of an Upside-Down Life." *Christian Parenting Today*, May/June 1999.

Parsons, Rob. "Almost Everything I Need to Know about God I Learned in Sunday School" (book excerpt). *Focus on the Family* magazine, February 2000.

Peters, Angie. *Celebrate Home*. St. Louis: Concordia Publishing House, 1998.

Peters, Paula. "Back on Track." *Cape Cod Times*, Section B, March 12, 2000.

Rausch, Thomas P. *Catholics and Evangelicals: Do They Share a Common Future?* Mahwah, New Jersey: Paulist Press, 2000.

Reed, Elizabeth Hoffman. *Gathering at the Table*. Chicago: Liturgy Training Publications, 1999.

Roiphe, Anne. *Fruitful*. New York: Houghton Mifflin Company, 1996.

Savage, Jill. *Professionalizing Motherhood*. Grand Rapids, Michigan: Zondervan Publishing House, 2001.

Schlessinger, Laura. *Parenthood by Proxy*. New York: HarperCollins Publishers, 2000.

Shriver, Maria. *Ten Things I Wish I'd Known—Before I Went Out into the Real World*. New York: Warner Books, 2000.

Simon, Mary Manz. "Surrounded by Stuff." *Christian Parenting Today*, May/June 1999.

Simon, Mary Manz. "Ask Dr. Mary." *Christian Parenting Today*, March/April 2000.

MAKING PEACE *with* MOTHERHOOD

Smolowe, Jill, Cynthia Wang, Marianne Stochmal, and Jane Podesta. "Mom on a mission." *People* magazine, June 19, 2000.

Stoddard, Alexandra. *Mothers, A Celebration.* New York: William Morrow and Company, 1996.

Talbot, John Michael with Dan O'Neil. *Simplicity.* Ann Arbor, Michigan: Servant Publications, 1989.

Tirabassi, Becky. *Being a Wild, Wonderful Woman for God.* Grand Rapids, Michigan: Zondervan Publishing House, 1994.

Tobias, Cynthia Ulrich. *The Way They Learn.* Colorado Springs, Colorado: Focus on the Family Publishing, 1994.

Wachtel, Paul L. *The Poverty of Affluence.* Philadelphia: New Society Publishers, 1989.

Weisling, Gwen. *Raising Kids on Purpose for the Fun of It.* Old Tappan, New Jersey: Fleming H. Revell Company, 1989.

Wilson, Ronald S. "Before Affirmative Action." *Brown Alumni Monthly*, March/April 2000.

"World Vision's 10 Urgent Issues List." *World Vision Today*, Spring 2000.

Yancey, Philip. *What's So Amazing About Grace?* Grand Rapids, Michigan: Zondervan Publishing House, 1997.

Yates, Susan Alexander. *And Then I Had Kids.* Grand Rapids, Michigan: Baker Books, 2001.

Zimney, Connie Fourre. *In Praise of Homemaking.* Notre Dame, Indiana: Ave Maria Press, 1984.